How to Become Rich

Crafted by Skriuwer

Copyright © 2024 by Skriuwer.

All rights reserved. No part of this book may be used or reproduced in any form whatsoever without written permission except in the case of brief quotations in critical articles or reviews.

For more information, contact : **kontakt@skriuwer.com** (www.skriuwer.com)

Table of Contents

CHAPTER 1: INTRODUCTION: THE JOURNEY TO PROSPERITY
1.1 Understanding the drive for wealth
1.2 The significance of a prosperity mindset
1.3 Overview of success principles

CHAPTER 2: ESTABLISHING SPECIFIC FINANCIAL OBJECTIVES
2.1 Defining your monetary goals
2.2 The necessity of precision in goal setting
2.3 Aligning objectives with personal values

CHAPTER 3: DEVELOPING UNSHAKEABLE CONFIDENCE
3.1 Building self-assurance in your capabilities
3.2 Overcoming doubt and limiting beliefs
3.3 The role of positive thinking in wealth building

CHAPTER 4: UTILIZING SELF-SUGGESTION TECHNIQUES
4.1 Grasping the concept of autosuggestion
4.2 Crafting potent affirmations for prosperity
4.3 Incorporating autosuggestion into daily life

CHAPTER 5: GAINING SPECIALIZED EXPERTISE
5.1 Identifying crucial knowledge areas for wealth
5.2 Strategies to acquire and enhance expertise
5.3 Leveraging skills to create financial opportunities

CHAPTER 6: APPLYING CREATIVE THINKING FOR WEALTH
6.1 The importance of innovation in financial success
6.2 Methods to stimulate and expand creativity
6.3 Turning ideas into profitable ventures

CHAPTER 7: FORMULATING AN EFFECTIVE ACTION PLAN
7.1 Steps to develop a realistic financial strategy
7.2 The importance of flexibility in planning
7.3 Executing and monitoring your financial strategy

CHAPTER 8: MAKING FIRM AND TIMELY DECISIONS
8.1 The impact of decisiveness on wealth accumulation
8.2 Enhancing decision-making abilities
8.3 Learning from past decisions

CHAPTER 9: BUILDING STEADFAST DETERMINATION
9.1 The role of persistence in achieving wealth
9.2 Overcoming challenges and staying motivated
9.3 Developing resilience through continuous effort

CHAPTER 10: CREATING A NETWORK OF SUCCESS PARTNERS
10.1 The value of a supportive professional network
10.2 Connecting with like-minded individuals
10.3 Collaborating for mutual financial advancement

CHAPTER 11: CHANNELING PERSONAL ENERGY INTO SUCCESS
11.1 Understanding energy's impact on productivity
11.2 Directing energy towards financial goals
11.3 Sustaining energy for long-term success

CHAPTER 12: ENGAGING THE SUBCONSCIOUS FOR ACHIEVEMENT
12.1 The subconscious mind's role in wealth
12.2 Programming the subconscious for success
12.3 Identifying and changing subconscious patterns

CHAPTER 13: ENHANCING MENTAL CAPABILITIES
13.1 Improving cognitive functions for better decisions
13.2 Techniques to boost focus and clarity
13.3 Applying mental sharpness to spot opportunities

CHAPTER 14: RELYING ON INTUITION IN FINANCIAL MATTERS
14.1 Understanding intuition's role in wealth building
14.2 Developing and trusting your intuitive sense
14.3 Balancing logic and instinct in choices
14.4 Recognizing and overcoming intuitive blocks
14.5 Applying intuition to seize opportunities

CHAPTER 15: OVERCOMING THE SIX MAJOR FEARS
15.1 Identifying the six common fears
15.2 Understanding the impact of fear on success
15.3 Strategies to conquer each fear
15.4 Developing a fearless mindset
15.5 Maintaining progress despite challenges

Chapter 1

THE JOURNEY TO PROSPERITY

Understanding the Drive for Wealth

The quest for wealth is a universal pursuit, deeply embedded in the human experience. From the dawn of civilization, individuals have sought resources to secure their survival, enhance their quality of life, and foster a sense of security. This innate aspiration for financial success is not merely about accumulating wealth for its own sake but is often tied to deeper psychological and societal factors that influence behavior and decision-making.

At its core, the drive for wealth encompasses a desire for freedom. Financial resources provide individuals with the autonomy to make choices, pursue passions, and create a lifestyle that aligns with their personal values and aspirations. This sense of freedom is particularly significant in modern society, where economic mobility and independence are often seen as indicators of success. The ability to travel, invest in education, or support charitable causes can be profoundly fulfilling, suggesting that the pursuit of wealth is intrinsically linked to self-actualization.

Moreover, the aspiration for financial success is influenced by societal norms and cultural narratives. In many cultures, wealth is equated with status, power, and respect. The portrayal of affluent individuals in media and literature often glorifies the lifestyles of the rich, creating aspirational figures that many strive to emulate. This societal framing can lead to the belief that financial success is a measure of one's worth, placing immense pressure on individuals to achieve wealth as a validation of their efforts and abilities.

However, while the drive for wealth can motivate individuals to strive for excellence and innovate, it is not without its complexities. The pursuit of financial success can sometimes lead to an unhealthy obsession, where the relentless quest for more undermines personal relationships, mental health, and overall well-being. It's crucial to recognize that the motivations behind the desire for wealth can vary significantly among individuals. For some, the drive is fueled by a desire for security and stability, while for others, it may stem from materialistic values or the need for societal approval.

Understanding this multifaceted drive for wealth also involves recognizing the implications of financial success on broader societal structures. Wealth inequality, for instance, can lead to social discord and hinder collective progress. The concentration of wealth in the hands of a few can create barriers for many, perpetuating cycles of poverty and limiting opportunities for upward mobility. Thus, the pursuit of wealth is not only a personal endeavor but a collective responsibility that requires ethical considerations and an awareness of its impact on the community.

Ultimately, the aspiration for financial success is a double-edged sword. It can serve as a powerful motivator that inspires individuals to achieve their goals and contribute positively to society. Conversely, if pursued without balance and consideration for its broader implications, it can lead to detrimental outcomes both personally and socially.

In conclusion, understanding the drive for wealth involves a nuanced exploration of human psychology, societal influences, and ethical responsibilities. By fostering a healthy perspective on financial success—one that values personal fulfillment and community well-being—individuals can align their aspirations with meaningful goals that transcend mere accumulation of resources, paving the way for a more equitable and prosperous society.

The Significance of a Prosperity Mindset

A prosperity mindset is a powerful catalyst for financial success, acting as the foundational belief system that shapes our approach to wealth creation. It encompasses a set of attitudes and beliefs that not only recognize the potential for abundance but also embrace the idea that financial success is achievable through deliberate actions and positive thinking. Understanding the significance of this mindset is crucial, as it influences not only our financial outcomes but also our overall approach to life and challenges.

At its core, a prosperity mindset shifts the focus from scarcity to abundance. Individuals with a scarcity mindset perceive resources, opportunities, and wealth as limited. This perspective can lead to feelings of fear and anxiety, stifling creativity and innovation. Conversely, those who adopt a prosperity mindset believe in the availability of resources and opportunities. This belief fosters an environment where individuals feel empowered to pursue their financial goals. By cultivating an abundance mentality, one can navigate challenges with optimism, viewing setbacks as temporary obstacles rather than insurmountable barriers.

A key component of the prosperity mindset is the belief in one's own ability to attract wealth. This self-efficacy is critical, as it influences the actions individuals take towards achieving their financial goals. When individuals believe that they can create their own financial success, they are more likely to take calculated risks, seek out opportunities, and invest in their personal and professional development. This proactive approach not only enhances their skill set but also increases their marketability and earning potential in various fields.

Additionally, adopting a prosperity mindset encourages resilience. The journey towards financial success is often fraught with challenges and setbacks. However, individuals who maintain a positive outlook are more likely to persist through difficulties. They view failures as learning experiences, using them to refine their strategies and approaches. This resilience is essential for long-term success, as it enables individuals to remain focused on their goals despite temporary setbacks.

Moreover, a prosperity mindset fosters a sense of gratitude and appreciation for what one already has. This practice of gratitude can create a positive feedback loop, attracting more abundance into one's life. When individuals acknowledge and appreciate their current resources, they open themselves up to receiving more. This mindset can also enhance relationships, as people with a prosperity mindset tend to be more generous and supportive, contributing to a network of mutual success.

Furthermore, the influence of a prosperity mindset extends beyond personal finances; it can impact the broader community. Individuals who embrace this mindset are more likely to engage in philanthropy and contribute to causes that promote social and economic development. This creates a cycle of abundance, where the prosperity of one individual can lead to the prosperity of others, fostering a community-oriented approach to wealth.

In practice, cultivating a prosperity mindset involves consistent self-reflection and affirmation. Individuals can engage in practices such as visualization, journaling, and meditation to reinforce their beliefs in abundance and their capacity for success. By regularly reminding themselves of their goals and envisioning their success, they strengthen their resolve and commitment to achieving financial prosperity.

In conclusion, the significance of a prosperity mindset cannot be overstated. It serves as the driving force behind financial success, shaping how individuals perceive opportunities, tackle challenges, and interact with their environment. By embracing an abundance mentality, cultivating resilience, and fostering gratitude, individuals position themselves to not only achieve their financial goals but also contribute positively to their communities. In this way, the journey towards wealth becomes not just a personal endeavor but a shared experience of growth and abundance.

Overview of Success Principles

In the journey toward financial prosperity, understanding and embracing certain core principles is paramount. These principles serve as the foundation upon which a robust financial strategy can be built and will be elaborated upon in subsequent chapters. By internalizing these success principles, individuals can navigate the complexities of wealth-building with clarity and purpose.

1. The Prosperity Mindset
At the heart of financial success lies the prosperity mindset—a way of thinking that embraces abundance rather than scarcity. This principle emphasizes the importance of seeing opportunities where others see obstacles. Cultivating a mindset oriented toward growth allows individuals to remain open to new possibilities, fostering a sense of optimism that is crucial for overcoming challenges. In subsequent chapters, we will delve deeper into how a

prosperity-focused mindset can significantly influence financial outcomes.

2. Goal Setting

The second principle revolves around the necessity of setting clear, specific financial goals. Without defined objectives, efforts can become aimless and unfocused. This principle underscores the importance of articulating measurable goals that guide actions and decisions. In later sections, we will explore techniques for effective goal-setting, including aligning these objectives with personal values to ensure that the pursuit of wealth is not only profitable but also fulfilling.

3. Confidence and Self-Belief

Developing unshakeable confidence is another critical principle of success. Financial pursuits often come with risks, and the ability to trust in one's capabilities is essential for navigating these uncertainties. This principle will be discussed in detail, including strategies for overcoming self-doubt and limiting beliefs that can obstruct the path to wealth. A positive self-image fosters resilience and empowers individuals to take bold steps toward their financial aspirations.

4. Continuous Learning and Expertise

In an ever-evolving financial landscape, gaining specialized knowledge is essential. This principle emphasizes the importance of identifying key areas of expertise that can lead to wealth. We will explore practical strategies for acquiring and enhancing skills, as well as how to leverage this knowledge to create financial opportunities. The pursuit of expertise is a lifelong journey that can significantly elevate one's potential for success.

5. Action Orientation

Another fundamental principle is the importance of formulating and executing an effective action plan. Financial success requires more than just planning; it demands action. This principle will guide readers through the process of developing realistic financial strategies, highlighting the need for flexibility in planning as circumstances change. The ability to execute and monitor one's plan will be addressed, emphasizing the significance of adaptability in the pursuit of wealth.

6. Decisiveness

Timely and firm decision-making is a cornerstone of wealth accumulation. This principle highlights how the ability to make prompt decisions can lead to significant financial advantages. In the following chapters, we will discuss techniques to enhance decision-making abilities and the importance of learning from past experiences to inform future choices.

7. Networking and Collaboration

Building a network of success partners is essential in today's interconnected world. Relationships can have a profound impact on financial outcomes, and this principle encourages readers to connect with like-minded individuals who can support their wealth-building goals. Strategies for collaboration and mutual advancement will be explored, showcasing the power of synergy in achieving financial success.

8. Resilience and Determination

Lastly, steadfast determination and resilience are vital in the face of challenges. This principle emphasizes maintaining motivation and persistence, even when obstacles arise. The ability to cultivate resilience through continuous effort will be examined, providing readers with the tools to stay committed to their financial goals.

In summary, these core principles serve as a roadmap for individuals seeking to achieve financial success. By understanding and applying these principles, readers will be better equipped to navigate their journey toward wealth, laying the groundwork for the detailed discussions that follow in this comprehensive guide.

Chapter 2

ESTABLISHING SPECIFIC FINANCIAL OBJECTIVES

Defining Your Monetary Goals

Defining monetary goals is a crucial step in the journey towards financial independence and prosperity. Without clear objectives, the path to wealth can feel overwhelming and aimless. To navigate this journey effectively, it is essential to articulate specific and measurable financial goals that provide direction and motivation. This section will guide you through the process of defining these goals, ensuring they align with your broader aspirations and values.

Understanding the Importance of Specificity

When setting financial goals, specificity is paramount. Generalized goals, such as "I want to be rich," lack clarity and fail to provide a roadmap for action. Instead, consider framing your goals in concrete terms. For instance, rather than stating "I want to save money," articulate a specific amount, such as "I want to save $10,000 for a down payment on a house within the next two years." This level of detail not only clarifies the target but also establishes a measurable benchmark for success.

The SMART Criteria

To enhance the effectiveness of your financial goals, consider utilizing the SMART criteria—Specific, Measurable, Achievable, Relevant, and Time-bound. Each element plays a vital role in ensuring that your goals are well-structured:

1. **Specific**: Clearly define what you want to achieve. Instead of "I want to be debt-free," specify "I want to pay off my credit card debt of $5,000 within 12 months."

2. **Measurable**: Establish criteria for measuring your progress. This could include tracking your savings, income growth, or debt reduction. For example, "I will save $500 each month until I reach my $10,000 target."

3. **Achievable**: Ensure that your goals are realistic and attainable. While it's essential to aim high, setting unattainable goals can lead to frustration and discouragement. Assess your current financial situation and capabilities to determine what is feasible.

4. **Relevant**: Align your goals with your broader financial aspirations and personal values. A goal should resonate with your long-term vision. For example, if financial independence is your ultimate aim, ensure that your goals contribute to that vision.

5. **Time-bound**: Assign a deadline to your goals to create a sense of urgency and accountability. This could involve setting short-term, medium-term, and long-term goals. A short-term goal may be saving for a vacation, while a long-term goal could be retirement savings.

Breaking Down Goals into Actionable Steps

Once you have defined your monetary goals using the SMART framework, the next step is to break them down into actionable steps. Each goal can be overwhelming if viewed as a whole, but dividing it into smaller, manageable tasks makes the process more approachable. For example, if your goal is to save $10,000 in two years, break it down into monthly savings targets and identify specific actions to achieve those targets, such as reducing discretionary spending or finding additional income sources.

Regular Review and Adjustment

Financial goals are not static; they should evolve with your changing circumstances and aspirations. Regularly review your goals and assess your progress. This practice allows you to adjust your strategies as needed and ensures that your goals remain relevant to your life situation. If you encounter obstacles, reflect on what adjustments can be made, whether it's altering your timeline or revising your savings strategies.

Conclusion

Defining clear, specific, and measurable monetary goals is a foundational step in the journey towards financial prosperity. By utilizing the SMART criteria, breaking down goals into actionable steps, and committing to regular review and adjustment, you can create a structured approach to achieving financial success. As you embark on this journey, remember that each small step brings you closer to your ultimate financial aspirations.

The Necessity of Precision in Goal Setting

Setting financial goals is a critical step in the journey toward wealth creation, but the effectiveness of these goals hinges significantly on their clarity and precision. Vague aspirations such as "I want to be rich" or "I hope to save more money" lack the specific direction that can guide an individual toward actionable steps. To truly harness the power of goal setting, one must understand the necessity of precision in articulating financial objectives.

Why Precision Matters

Precise goals serve as a roadmap, providing clear direction and purpose. When goals are specific, they eliminate ambiguity, making it easier to determine the necessary actions to achieve them. For instance, stating "I want to save $10,000 for a house down payment within two years" is far more effective than simply saying "I want to save money." This specificity not only clarifies the end target but also establishes a timeline, allowing for the development of a structured plan with measurable milestones along the way.

Moreover, precise goals help track progress. When goals are defined in quantifiable terms, individuals can monitor their advancements and make necessary adjustments. For example, breaking down a larger goal into smaller, monthly savings targets—like "I will save $500 each month"—enables a person to evaluate their performance regularly and identify if they are on track or need to recalibrate their efforts.

SMART Goals Framework

One effective method for establishing precise financial goals is the SMART criteria—Specific, Measurable, Achievable, Relevant, and Time-bound. Each element of this framework enhances the clarity and effectiveness of goal setting:

1. Specific: Clearly define what you want to achieve. For instance, instead of general goals like "increase income," specify "earn an additional $5,000 through freelance work."

2. Measurable: Ensure that your goal can be quantified. This could mean specifying a dollar amount saved, a percentage increase in income, or a defined number of investments made.

3. Achievable: While ambition is important, goals should be realistic. Setting a goal to save $100,000 in six months may be admirable but could lead to frustration if it is unattainable.

4. Relevant: Goals should align with personal values and long-term aspirations, ensuring that the pursuit of these objectives is meaningful and motivating.

5. Time-bound: Establishing a deadline creates a sense of urgency, prompting action. A well-defined timeframe can also help in prioritizing tasks and managing time effectively.

Aligning Goals with Financial Planning
Precision in goal setting also enhances financial planning. When financial goals are clear, they can be integrated into a comprehensive financial strategy that includes budgeting, investing, and saving. For example, if your goal is to retire with a nest egg of $1 million by age 65, you can work backward to determine how much you need to save each month, the types of investments suitable for your risk tolerance, and other financial strategies that align with your objectives.

Avoiding Common Pitfalls
One of the common pitfalls in goal setting is setting overly broad or unrealistic goals, which can lead to disillusionment and eventual abandonment of financial pursuits. By emphasizing precision, individuals can create a more sustainable approach to wealth building, minimizing the likelihood of frustration and disappointment.

In conclusion, the necessity of precision in goal setting cannot be overstated. Clear, specific, and measurable financial goals serve as the foundation for effective financial planning and wealth accumulation. They enable individuals to track their progress, adjust their strategies as necessary, and maintain motivation throughout their financial journey. By adopting a disciplined approach to goal setting, individuals can empower themselves to transform their aspirations into tangible financial success.

Aligning Objectives with Personal Values

In the pursuit of wealth, it is crucial to ensure that financial objectives resonate deeply with your core beliefs and values. This alignment is not merely a philosophical exercise; it is essential for sustainable success and personal fulfillment. When your financial goals are congruent with your values, you are more likely to remain motivated, focused, and resilient in the face of obstacles. This section explores the importance of aligning financial objectives with personal values and provides strategies to achieve this alignment.

Understanding Personal Values

Personal values are the guiding principles that shape your beliefs, decisions, and behaviors. They encompass what you consider essential in life, such as integrity, family, health, freedom, security, and community. To determine your core values, consider reflecting on the following questions:

- What principles do you prioritize in your life?
- What gives you a sense of purpose and fulfillment?
- In what areas do you feel most strongly about making an impact?

Once you have identified your core values, the next step is to assess how they influence your financial aspirations. For example, if one of your primary values is community service, your financial goals may focus on generating wealth that enables you to contribute to charitable causes or support local initiatives.

The Importance of Alignment

Aligning financial objectives with personal values offers several advantages:

1. Increased Motivation: When your financial goals reflect what you genuinely care about, you are more likely to pursue them with passion and commitment. This intrinsic motivation can sustain you through difficulties and challenges.

2. Enhanced Decision-Making: Clarity around your values provides a framework for making informed financial decisions. When faced with choices, you can evaluate options based on whether they are in harmony with your values, leading to more satisfying outcomes.

3. Long-Term Satisfaction: Financial success that is achieved without regard for personal values may lead to feelings of emptiness or discontent. In contrast, aligning your wealth-building efforts with your values fosters a sense of fulfillment and purpose, creating a more meaningful journey toward financial independence.

4. Resilience Against Setbacks: The path to wealth is often fraught with challenges. When your goals resonate with your personal values, you are better equipped to navigate setbacks and maintain a positive outlook, as you remain focused on the bigger picture of what you want to achieve.

Strategies for Alignment

To ensure that your financial objectives are aligned with your values, consider the following strategies:

1. Reflect and Write: Take time to articulate your core values on paper. Reflect on how each value translates into specific financial objectives. For instance, if you value security, your objectives may include building an emergency fund or saving for retirement.

2. Set Value-Driven Goals: When defining your financial goals, ensure they directly relate to your values. For example, if you value family, you might set a goal to save for a family vacation or invest in a home that accommodates your loved ones.

3. Regular Review and Adjustments: Periodically review your financial objectives to ensure they continue to align with your evolving values. Life circumstances change, and so may your priorities. Adjust your goals accordingly to maintain that harmony.

4. Seek Professional Guidance: If you find it challenging to align your financial objectives with your values, consider working with a financial advisor or coach. They can provide insights and strategies tailored to your unique situation, helping you create a roadmap that reflects both your financial aspirations and your core beliefs.

In conclusion, aligning your financial objectives with your personal values is a vital step in the wealth-building journey. It fosters intrinsic motivation, enhances decision-making, and cultivates long-term satisfaction. By taking the time to reflect on your values and ensuring your financial goals resonate with them, you pave the way for not just monetary success but also a richer, more fulfilling life.

Chapter 3

DEVELOPING UNSHAKEABLE CONFIDENCE

Building Self-Assurance in Your Capabilities

Self-assurance is a fundamental pillar in the journey toward wealth. It represents an unwavering belief in one's skills, knowledge, and capacity to achieve financial success. Developing this self-assurance is crucial, as it empowers individuals to take bold steps, make informed decisions, and navigate the inevitable challenges associated with wealth-building. Here, we explore actionable strategies to cultivate self-assurance, enhancing one's confidence in their capabilities.

1. Self-Assessment and Acknowledgment of Strengths
The first step in building self-assurance is a thorough self-assessment. Take the time to identify and acknowledge your strengths, skills, and past achievements. Reflect on experiences where you excelled or overcame significant challenges. Document these instances, as keeping a record of your successes can serve as a powerful reminder of your capabilities. This acknowledgment not only boosts confidence but also reinforces the belief that you possess the necessary skills to achieve your financial goals.

2. Setting Achievable Goals
Goal setting is a critical component of developing self-assurance. Start by setting small, achievable goals that are aligned with your broader financial objectives. Achieving these smaller milestones provides a sense of accomplishment and reinforces your belief in your abilities. For instance, if your ultimate goal is to start a

business, begin by setting a goal to conduct market research or develop a business plan. Celebrate each achievement, no matter how minor, as it contributes to building your overall confidence.

3. Continuous Learning and Skill Development

Investing in personal development is essential for enhancing self-assurance. Engage in continuous learning by taking courses, attending workshops, or seeking mentorship in areas relevant to your financial aspirations. This not only expands your knowledge base but also reinforces your belief in your ability to learn and grow. When you are equipped with the right tools and information, you naturally become more confident in your decision-making processes.

4. Surrounding Yourself with Supportive Influences

The company you keep significantly influences your self-assurance. Surround yourself with positive, supportive individuals who encourage your ambitions and provide constructive feedback. This network can include mentors, peers, or even family members who believe in your potential. Engaging with like-minded individuals fosters a sense of community and can provide additional motivation, enabling you to reinforce your self-belief.

5. Practicing Positive Self-Talk

The language we use when speaking to ourselves plays a crucial role in shaping our self-assurance. Practice positive self-talk by replacing negative or self-doubting thoughts with affirmations that reinforce your capabilities. For example, instead of thinking, "I can't manage my finances," reframe it to, "I am learning to manage my finances effectively." This shift in mindset can have profound effects on your self-perception and overall confidence.

6. Embracing Failure as a Learning Opportunity
Fear of failure often undermines self-assurance. To combat this, reframe your perspective on failure. Instead of viewing it as a setback, see it as a valuable learning opportunity. Analyze what went wrong, extract lessons from the experience, and apply these insights to future endeavors. Embracing failure as part of the journey fosters resilience, enabling you to approach challenges with renewed confidence.

7. Visualization Techniques
Visualization is a powerful technique to enhance self-assurance. Spend time visualizing yourself achieving your financial goals and experiencing the emotions associated with that success. This mental imagery reinforces your belief in your capabilities and prepares you to take action toward your aspirations.

In conclusion, building self-assurance in your capabilities requires intentional effort and a commitment to personal growth. By conducting self-assessments, setting achievable goals, investing in learning, fostering supportive relationships, practicing positive self-talk, embracing failure, and utilizing visualization techniques, you can cultivate the confidence necessary to pursue and attain wealth. Remember, self-assurance is not a destination but an ongoing journey of growth and empowerment.

Overcoming Doubt and Limiting Beliefs
In the pursuit of wealth, one of the most formidable obstacles individuals face is the internal dialogue that fosters doubt and reinforces limiting beliefs. These mental barriers can significantly impede financial success, often manifesting as self-sabotage, hesitation, or a paralysis of action. To overcome these challenges, it

is essential to first identify the nature of these doubts and beliefs, then implement strategies to dismantle them effectively.

Identifying Doubt and Limiting Beliefs
Doubt often arises from past experiences, societal conditioning, or negative feedback from others. It can take various forms, such as the fear of failure, the belief that one is not deserving of wealth, or the perception that financial success is unattainable. Common limiting beliefs include thoughts like "I am not good with money," "Wealth is for others, not for me," or "I'll never be able to start that business." These beliefs create a mental barrier that hinders individuals from taking actionable steps towards their financial goals.

The first step in overcoming these doubts is self-reflection. Journaling can be a powerful tool for this process. By writing down thoughts and feelings about money, wealth, and success, individuals can identify recurring themes and patterns that indicate limiting beliefs. Once these patterns are recognized, the next step is to challenge their validity. Are these beliefs based on facts, or are they assumptions rooted in fear and uncertainty?

Addressing Mental Barriers
To combat doubt and limiting beliefs, individuals can employ several strategies:

1. Reframing Thoughts: This involves changing the narrative surrounding one's beliefs about wealth. Instead of thinking, "I am not good with money," a more empowering statement would be, "I am learning to manage my finances effectively." This shift in perspective can alter the emotional response to financial situations, fostering a sense of empowerment rather than helplessness.

2. Affirmations: Positive affirmations can help reinforce a mindset conducive to financial success. By regularly repeating affirmations such as "I am capable of achieving my financial goals" or "I attract wealth effortlessly," individuals can begin to rewire their subconscious beliefs about money. This practice encourages a proactive mindset and diminishes the power of negative thoughts.

3. Visualization: Visualization techniques can be instrumental in overcoming doubt. By vividly imagining the desired outcome—whether it's achieving a specific financial goal or living a life of abundance—individuals can create a mental image that aligns with their aspirations. This not only boosts confidence but also serves as a motivational tool to take actionable steps toward those goals.

4. Seeking Support: Surrounding oneself with positive influences can significantly impact one's mindset. Engaging with mentors, coaches, or supportive networks can provide encouragement and accountability. These relationships can offer new perspectives and insights, helping to dismantle limiting beliefs and replace them with constructive feedback and motivation.

5. Taking Small Steps: Building confidence often requires action. Start by setting small, achievable financial goals and gradually increase the complexity of these goals as confidence builds. Each success reinforces the belief that financial success is attainable, further diminishing doubt and limiting beliefs.

6. **Embracing Failure**: Understanding that failure is a natural part of the journey toward success can alleviate the fear associated with taking risks. By viewing failures as learning experiences rather than reflections of self-worth, individuals can foster resilience and a growth mindset that propels them forward.

Conclusion
Overcoming doubt and limiting beliefs is a crucial step on the journey to financial success. By identifying these mental barriers, reframing thoughts, utilizing affirmations, visualizing success, seeking support, taking proactive steps, and embracing failure, individuals can cultivate a mindset that not only acknowledges their worthiness of wealth but actively pursues it. This transformation in thought patterns is essential for unlocking the potential for financial growth and prosperity.

The Role of Positive Thinking in Wealth Building

In the journey toward financial prosperity, the significance of a positive mindset cannot be overstated. Positive thinking serves as a powerful catalyst for wealth creation, influencing not only how individuals perceive their financial circumstances but also how they respond to challenges and opportunities. At its core, positive thinking involves maintaining an optimistic outlook and focusing on constructive outcomes, which can lead to a multitude of benefits for aspiring wealth builders.

Shaping Financial Perspectives
The way we think about money fundamentally shapes our financial behaviors and decisions. A positive mindset allows individuals to approach financial challenges with a solution-oriented perspective. Instead of succumbing to fear or paralysis in the face of financial difficulties, those with a positive outlook are more likely to view

obstacles as opportunities for growth. This shift in perspective encourages proactive behavior, leading to better financial planning and decision-making.

Moreover, positive thinking is closely linked to self-efficacy—the belief in one's ability to succeed. When individuals cultivate a belief that they can achieve their financial goals, they are more likely to take calculated risks and pursue opportunities that align with their aspirations. This self-belief fosters resilience, enabling individuals to bounce back from setbacks and maintain momentum toward their financial objectives.

Enhancing Motivation and Drive
Positive thinking also plays a crucial role in sustaining motivation and drive. Wealth-building is often a long-term endeavor that requires consistent effort, discipline, and perseverance. A positive mindset fuels intrinsic motivation, making the pursuit of financial goals more enjoyable and fulfilling. When individuals focus on what they can achieve rather than the limitations they face, they are more likely to engage in behaviors that promote financial growth—such as investing in their education, seeking new opportunities, and networking with others who share similar ambitions.

Furthermore, positive thinking can mitigate feelings of stress and anxiety associated with financial uncertainties. When individuals maintain a hopeful outlook, they are less likely to be paralyzed by fear or overwhelmed by negative emotions. This emotional resilience allows them to navigate the complexities of wealth building with greater ease and confidence.

Attracting Opportunities
The Law of Attraction, a popular concept in personal development, posits that positive thoughts can attract positive experiences. While this idea may seem abstract, there is a psychological basis for it. A positive mindset can enhance one's ability to notice and seize opportunities that others may overlook. Individuals who believe in their capacity for success are more likely to take action, engage in networking, and pursue ventures that can lead to financial advancement.

Additionally, a positive attitude can influence how others perceive and interact with an individual. People are naturally drawn to those who exude positivity and confidence. This magnetism can lead to valuable connections, partnerships, and collaborations that can further enhance financial prospects.

Cultivating a Positive Mindset
To harness the benefits of positive thinking in wealth building, individuals can adopt specific practices that foster an optimistic outlook. These may include:

1. Gratitude Journaling: Regularly reflecting on and writing down things one is grateful for can shift focus from scarcity to abundance, reinforcing a positive mindset.

2. Positive Affirmations: Repeating affirmations that emphasize financial success and self-worth can reshape one's beliefs and attitudes toward wealth.

3. Visualization: Imagining oneself achieving financial goals can create a mental blueprint for success, instilling confidence and motivation.

4. Surrounding Oneself with Positivity: Engaging with positive influences, whether through books, podcasts, or uplifting social circles, can bolster an optimistic outlook.

In summary, a positive mindset is not just a feel-good notion but a critical component of wealth building. By fostering optimism, individuals can enhance their financial decision-making, maintain motivation, attract opportunities, and ultimately pave the way toward achieving their financial aspirations. Embracing positivity is a transformative step on the path to prosperity, enabling individuals to navigate the financial landscape with confidence and resilience.

Chapter 4

UTILIZING SELF-SUGGESTION TECHNIQUES

Grasping the Concept of Autosuggestion

Autosuggestion is a psychological technique that involves using self-induced suggestions to influence one's beliefs and behaviors. This concept, popularized by the French psychologist Émile Coué in the early 20th century, is based on the premise that by repeating positive affirmations or suggestions, individuals can alter their subconscious thought processes, thereby impacting their emotions, actions, and ultimately, their outcomes. Understanding autosuggestion is crucial for anyone aspiring to achieve prosperity, as the subconscious mind plays a pivotal role in shaping our financial realities and overall success.

At its core, autosuggestion operates on the principle that the subconscious mind is highly receptive to repetitive thoughts and affirmations. Unlike the conscious mind, which is analytical and skeptical, the subconscious mind absorbs information more passively and is less critical of what it accepts as truth. This characteristic makes it particularly susceptible to suggestions that are repeated frequently and with conviction. For instance, if an individual continuously asserts, "I am capable of achieving financial abundance," this affirmation can gradually seep into their subconscious, fostering a belief in their ability to generate wealth.

The influence of autosuggestion on the subconscious mind can be profound. By consciously choosing positive affirmations, individuals can reprogram their subconscious beliefs, replacing limiting thoughts with empowering ones. This process is particularly important in the context of financial success, where limiting beliefs—such as "I don't deserve wealth" or "Money is hard to come by"—can hinder one's ability to pursue and achieve monetary goals. By employing autosuggestion, individuals can counteract these negative beliefs, fostering a mindset that is conducive to wealth creation.

To effectively utilize autosuggestion, it is essential to craft affirmations that resonate personally and are framed in the present tense. For example, rather than saying, "I will be wealthy," a more impactful affirmation would be, "I am attracting wealth into my life." The present tense creates a sense of immediacy and reinforces the belief that financial abundance is already part of one's reality. Additionally, affirmations should be specific and actionable, such as, "I am diligently saving and investing my money to build a secure financial future."

Incorporating autosuggestion into daily life requires consistency and commitment. Here are several effective methods to practice autosuggestion:

1. Daily Affirmation Rituals: Set aside a few minutes each day to repeat your chosen affirmations aloud or in writing. Morning rituals can be particularly effective, as they set a positive tone for the day.

2. Visual Reminders: Write your affirmations on sticky notes and place them in prominent locations—such as on mirrors, computer screens, or refrigerator doors—where you will see them frequently. This constant visual reinforcement helps to embed the affirmations into your subconscious.

3. Meditation and Visualization: Integrate your affirmations into meditation sessions. Visualize yourself achieving your financial goals while repeating your affirmations, creating a powerful mental image that strengthens your belief in their possibility.

4. Positive Environment: Surround yourself with supportive people who encourage your financial aspirations. Their positive reinforcement can enhance the effectiveness of your autosuggestion practices.

The ultimate goal of autosuggestion is to cultivate a mindset that aligns with one's financial objectives, enabling individuals to navigate challenges and seize opportunities with confidence. By harnessing the power of autosuggestion, individuals can create a self-fulfilling prophecy, where their beliefs about wealth and success align with their actions, leading to tangible financial outcomes. In this way, the practice of autosuggestion becomes a fundamental tool for anyone on the journey to financial prosperity, guiding them toward the realization of their wealth-building potential.

Crafting Potent Affirmations for Prosperity

Affirmations are powerful tools that can significantly influence our mindset, beliefs, and ultimately, our financial outcomes. When crafted effectively, affirmations can reinforce our aspirations for prosperity and help to align our subconscious mind with our conscious goals. This section outlines practical guidelines for creating potent affirmations that can propel you towards financial success.

1. Be Specific and Clear
The first step in crafting effective affirmations is to ensure they are specific and clear. Vague statements like "I want to be rich" lack the precision necessary for the subconscious mind to act upon. Instead, articulate exactly what wealth means to you. For example, "I am attracting $100,000 in my savings account by the end of this year" is a clear and measurable affirmation. Specificity helps to create a vivid mental image, making it easier for your mind to focus on the desired outcome.

2. Use Present Tense
Affirmations should be phrased in the present tense, as if the desired outcome is already happening. This approach helps to cultivate a mindset of abundance and helps to bypass the mental barriers that can arise when we frame our goals in the future tense. Instead of saying "I will be financially free," say "I am financially free." This shift in phrasing sends a message to your subconscious that the desired state is a current reality, thereby enhancing your belief in its attainment.

3. Incorporate Positive Language
When crafting affirmations, use positive language that emphasizes what you want, rather than what you don't want. Negative phrasing can create confusion and undermine your intentions. For instance, instead of saying "I am no longer in debt," reframe it as "I am financially abundant and free from debt." This positive framing not only reinforces your aspirations but also helps to cultivate a mindset centered around growth and potential.

4. Make It Personal
Your affirmations should reflect your personal values, beliefs, and aspirations. Tailor them to resonate with your individual

circumstances and what wealth means to you. For instance, if you value security and comfort, you might say, "I am creating a comfortable and secure financial future for myself and my family." Personalization makes your affirmations more meaningful and relevant, increasing their potency.

5. Infuse Emotion
For affirmations to be truly effective, they must evoke a sense of emotion. When you repeat your affirmations, try to connect with the feelings associated with achieving the desired outcome. Visualize the joy, excitement, and freedom that financial prosperity brings. Phrasing like "I am joyfully embracing my financial abundance" conveys not just the affirmation but also the emotional state you wish to embody.

6. Repeat Regularly
Repetition is key to embedding affirmations into your subconscious. Create a daily routine where you can recite your affirmations, such as in the morning as you wake up or at night before you go to sleep. Consider writing them down and placing them in visible locations such as your workspace or bathroom mirror. The more frequently you engage with your affirmations, the more they become a part of your thought patterns.

7. Visualize and Act
Affirmations are most effective when paired with visualization and action. As you recite your affirmations, take a moment to visualize the life you desire. Picture yourself living in abundance, making sound financial decisions, and experiencing the joy that wealth brings. Furthermore, take actionable steps towards your financial goals to reinforce the beliefs you are cultivating. Action solidifies the connection between your affirmations and tangible results.

In conclusion, crafting potent affirmations for prosperity involves specificity, present tense, positive language, personalization, emotional connection, repetition, visualization, and action. By integrating these guidelines into your affirmation practice, you can cultivate a mindset that supports your financial aspirations, enabling you to manifest the wealth you desire.

Incorporating Autosuggestion into Daily Life

Autosuggestion, a concept popularized by the psychologist Émile Coué, refers to the practice of influencing one's own subconscious mind through repeated affirmations or suggestions. By harnessing the power of autosuggestion, individuals can cultivate a positive mindset, reinforce their financial goals, and ultimately create pathways to wealth. The effectiveness of autosuggestion lies in its ability to reprogram the subconscious, which often dictates our beliefs, perceptions, and reactions to challenges. Here are several methods to incorporate self-suggestion practices into your daily life:

1. Create Powerful Affirmations

The first step in integrating autosuggestion into daily life is to craft personalized affirmations. These affirmations should be positive, present tense statements that resonate with your financial aspirations. For example, rather than stating "I want to be rich," a more effective affirmation would be "I am attracting wealth and opportunities effortlessly." This subtle shift in language reinforces the belief that wealth is not just a desire; it is an ongoing reality. Aim to create a list of five to ten affirmations that reflect your financial goals, ensuring they evoke positive emotions and motivation.

2. Daily Repetition

Once you have established your affirmations, the next step is daily repetition. This practice can be integrated seamlessly into your routine. Consider reciting your affirmations each morning when you wake up and each evening before you go to bed. This timing is particularly effective as your mind is transitioning into and out of sleep, making it more receptive to suggestion. You might also choose to write your affirmations down in a journal or display them prominently in your living space, such as on your mirror or fridge, to reinforce their significance visually throughout the day.

3. Visualization Techniques

Pairing affirmations with visualization can enhance the effectiveness of your autosuggestion practice. Visualization involves imagining yourself achieving your financial goals as vividly and realistically as possible. For instance, picture yourself living in your dream home, enjoying the lifestyle your wealth affords, or experiencing the satisfaction of financial independence. Engaging multiple senses during this visualization—such as feeling the texture of money, hearing the sounds of financial success, or even smelling the air of a luxurious environment—can make the experience more impactful. Set aside a few moments each day to immerse yourself in this visualization, ideally while in a calm state of mind.

4. Incorporate into Daily Routines

Integrate autosuggestion into everyday activities. For example, while commuting, listen to recordings of your affirmations or motivational audiobooks focused on wealth and success. During mundane tasks, such as cleaning or exercising, use this time to repeat your affirmations mentally or aloud. This not only reinforces your financial goals but also transforms routine activities into opportunities for self-improvement and motivation.

5. Mindfulness and Meditation

Practicing mindfulness and meditation can further enhance your autosuggestion efforts. Dedicate time to quiet your mind and focus on your affirmations in a meditative state. This deep focus allows you to connect with your subconscious more effectively, planting the seeds of your financial aspirations. Guided meditations that focus on wealth and abundance can also be beneficial, as they provide a structured approach to aligning your thoughts with your goals.

6. Track Progress and Adjust

Finally, keeping a journal to document your experiences with autosuggestion can provide valuable insights. Record your feelings, any shifts in mindset, and the progress you make towards your financial goals. This reflection can help you recognize patterns and adjust your affirmations as necessary to ensure they remain relevant and inspiring.

Incorporating autosuggestion into daily life is a powerful tool for personal growth and financial success. By consistently applying these methods, you can cultivate a mindset that not only attracts wealth but also empowers you to take proactive steps towards achieving your financial aspirations.

Chapter 5

GAINING SPECIALIZED EXPERTISE

Identifying Crucial Knowledge Areas for Wealth

Achieving financial success requires more than just ambition; it necessitates a well-rounded understanding of various knowledge areas that underpin wealth creation. Identifying these crucial domains not only equips individuals with the skills necessary to navigate the financial landscape but also empowers them to make informed decisions that lead to sustainable prosperity. Here, we explore key knowledge areas that aspiring wealth builders should focus on to enhance their financial literacy and effectiveness.

1. Financial Literacy

At the core of wealth creation lies financial literacy, which encompasses the understanding of fundamental financial principles such as budgeting, saving, investing, and debt management. Knowledge in this area allows individuals to make sound financial decisions, such as determining how much to save each month, understanding interest rates, and evaluating investment opportunities. A strong foundation in financial literacy enables individuals to interpret financial statements, assess risks, and recognize the implications of their financial choices.

2. Investment Strategies

Understanding investment strategies is crucial for building wealth over time. This knowledge area includes familiarity with different asset classes—stocks, bonds, real estate, and alternative investments—as well as the principles of diversification, risk assessment, and asset allocation. Aspiring wealth builders should learn about various investment vehicles and their respective risks and returns, allowing them to construct a balanced portfolio that aligns with their financial goals and risk tolerance. Knowledge of market trends and economic indicators can further enhance one's ability to make strategic investment decisions.

3. Entrepreneurship and Business Acumen
For many, entrepreneurship is a pathway to wealth. Developing business acumen involves understanding how to identify market opportunities, create business plans, and manage operations effectively. Knowledge in areas such as marketing, sales, and customer relationship management is essential for driving business success. Aspiring entrepreneurs should also be versed in financial management principles specific to businesses, including cash flow analysis, pricing strategies, and profit margin optimization. This knowledge not only helps in starting a business but also in scaling it effectively.

4. Taxation and Legal Considerations
An often-overlooked area in wealth-building is the understanding of taxation and legal considerations. Knowledge of tax laws, deductions, and credits can significantly impact one's financial outcomes. Wealth builders should be aware of the implications of capital gains tax, estate tax, and other tax-related issues that can affect wealth accumulation. Additionally, understanding legal structures for business entities, intellectual property rights, and contracts can protect wealth and ensure compliance, preventing costly legal issues down the road.

5. Personal Development and Soft Skills
Wealth creation is not solely about hard financial skills; personal development and soft skills play a pivotal role. Skills such as negotiation, effective communication, and networking are essential for building relationships that can lead to financial opportunities. Moreover, cultivating emotional intelligence enhances decision-making and resilience, enabling individuals to navigate the ups and downs of the wealth-building journey. Continuous learning and self-improvement are vital, as they keep individuals adaptable in an ever-changing economic landscape.

6. Economic Principles and Global Trends
A comprehensive understanding of economic principles and global trends is essential for making informed financial decisions. This includes knowledge of macroeconomic indicators, monetary policy, and the global economy's interconnectedness. Being informed about current events and how they influence markets can help wealth builders anticipate changes and adjust their strategies accordingly. Understanding economic cycles and their impact on investment opportunities can provide a competitive edge in wealth creation.

In conclusion, identifying and developing expertise in these crucial knowledge areas lays the groundwork for financial success. By focusing on financial literacy, investment strategies, entrepreneurship, taxation, personal development, and economic principles, individuals can equip themselves with the tools necessary to navigate the complex landscape of wealth-building effectively. This multifaceted approach not only enhances financial acumen but also fosters confidence and resilience, essential traits for achieving long-term prosperity.

Strategies to Acquire and Enhance Expertise

In today's rapidly changing economic landscape, the pursuit of wealth is often closely tied to specialized knowledge and expertise. To navigate this complex environment effectively, it is crucial to develop a strategic approach to acquiring and enhancing expertise in your chosen field. Below are several key strategies that can help you on this journey towards financial success.

1. Continuous Learning and Education:
One of the foundational strategies for gaining expertise is committing to continuous learning. This can take various forms, such as formal education, online courses, seminars, or workshops. Institutions like universities and professional organizations often offer courses that can deepen your understanding of specific subjects. Online platforms like Coursera, Udemy, or LinkedIn Learning provide access to a wide range of topics that can enhance your skills at your own pace. Additionally, reading industry-related books, journals, and articles can keep you informed about the latest trends and innovations, further enriching your knowledge base.

2. Networking and Collaboration:
Building a network of professionals within your area of interest is invaluable. Engaging in discussions and collaborations with peers can expose you to new perspectives and insights that can enhance your expertise. Attend industry conferences, join professional associations, and participate in local meetups to connect with like-minded individuals. By sharing knowledge and experiences, you not only learn from others but also establish relationships that can lead to mentorship opportunities and collaborative projects, which can provide practical experience and deeper insights into your field.

3. Practical Experience:

Hands-on experience is one of the most effective ways to acquire and enhance expertise. Seek opportunities to apply your knowledge in real-world scenarios. This could involve internships, volunteer work, or part-time jobs in your area of interest. By immersing yourself in the practical aspects of your field, you gain a clearer understanding of how theoretical concepts translate into practice. Additionally, projects or freelance work can further develop your skills while building a portfolio that showcases your capabilities.

4. Seeking Mentorship:

Finding a mentor who is an expert in your desired field can significantly accelerate your learning process. A mentor can provide personalized guidance, share valuable insights from their own experiences, and help you navigate challenges you may encounter along the way. Look for mentors through professional networks, alumni associations, or industry events. Establishing a mentor-mentee relationship can provide you with a supportive framework as you pursue your financial and professional goals.

5. Embracing Feedback and Self-Reflection:

Constructive criticism is essential for growth. Actively seek feedback from peers, mentors, and supervisors to identify areas of improvement. Embrace a mindset of self-reflection by regularly assessing your skills and knowledge. Ask yourself questions like: What have I learned recently? Where do I need to improve? This introspective approach will help you stay aware of your progress and identify specific areas to focus on for further development.

6. Specializing in a Niche:
While having a broad knowledge base can be beneficial, specializing in a niche area can set you apart in a competitive market. Identify a specific segment within your field that you are passionate about and focus your efforts on becoming an expert in that area. This focused approach allows you to develop in-depth knowledge and skills, making you a go-to resource in your niche.

7. Leveraging Technology:
Utilize technology to your advantage by accessing online forums, webinars, and educational resources that can enhance your expertise. Many industries have dedicated online communities where professionals share insights, challenges, and solutions. Engaging with these platforms can provide you with diverse perspectives and keep you updated on emerging trends.

By implementing these strategies, you can acquire and enhance your expertise, ultimately positioning yourself for greater financial success. The journey of learning is continuous, and the more proactive you are in your pursuit of knowledge, the more opportunities you will create for wealth-building in your chosen field.

Leveraging Skills to Create Financial Opportunities

In today's rapidly evolving economy, possessing specialized knowledge and skills is paramount to identifying and seizing financial opportunities. Expertise acts as a catalyst for innovation and entrepreneurship, enabling individuals to carve out niches in competitive markets. This section delves into how you can effectively leverage your skills to create wealth, providing actionable insights that can lead to financial success.

Understanding Your Unique Skill Set
The first step in leveraging skills is to conduct a thorough self-assessment. Identify your unique skills, experiences, and knowledge areas. These could range from technical skills in fields like coding, graphic design, or engineering, to soft skills such as negotiation, leadership, or communication. A clear understanding of what you excel at will not only boost your confidence but also help you recognize opportunities that align with your strengths.

Market Research: Spotting Opportunities
Once you have a solid grasp of your skills, the next step is market research. This involves examining current trends, consumer needs, and gaps in the market where your expertise can be beneficial. For instance, if you are a digital marketing specialist, you might notice a rising demand for local SEO services in your area. By staying informed through industry reports, online forums, and networking with other professionals, you can pinpoint potential opportunities that you can capitalize on.

Creating Value Through Specialized Knowledge
The essence of creating wealth lies in providing value. Utilize your specialized knowledge to develop products or services that address specific problems. For instance, if you are skilled in financial planning, consider offering workshops or one-on-one consulting sessions. Not only does this allow you to monetize your knowledge, but it also positions you as an authority in your field, attracting more clients and referrals.

Networking: Building Strategic Connections
Leveraging your skills isn't just about individual effort; it also involves connecting with others. Building a network of like-minded professionals can open doors to collaborations and partnerships.

Attend industry conferences, join professional organizations, and participate in online communities where you can share your expertise and learn from others. Networking can lead to joint ventures, referrals, and access to resources that can enhance your ability to create financial opportunities.

Continuous Learning and Skill Enhancement
The market is always changing, and staying relevant is crucial. Invest in continuous learning to enhance your existing skills or acquire new ones that complement your expertise. Online courses, certifications, and workshops are excellent avenues for skill development. By expanding your skill set, you not only increase your value in the job market but also broaden your scope for identifying and exploiting new financial opportunities.

Leveraging Technology
In the digital age, technology can significantly amplify your ability to leverage skills for financial gain. Utilize social media platforms, websites, and e-commerce tools to reach a wider audience. For instance, if you are a writer or content creator, platforms like Medium or YouTube can help you monetize your content while showcasing your expertise. Additionally, tools like LinkedIn can facilitate professional connections, making it easier to find opportunities tailored to your skills.

Taking Initiative: From Idea to Action
Finally, it's essential to take initiative. The most successful individuals are those who not only identify opportunities but also act on them. Develop a plan that outlines how you will use your skills to create financial opportunities. This could involve starting a side business, freelancing, or transitioning into a new career that

better utilizes your expertise. Set specific, measurable goals to keep yourself accountable and track your progress.

By methodically leveraging your specialized skills, conducting thorough market research, networking strategically, committing to lifelong learning, utilizing technology, and taking decisive action, you can effectively create and exploit financial opportunities. This proactive approach not only contributes to your personal wealth but also enriches the community and economy, fostering a cycle of continuous growth and success.

Chapter 6

APPLYING CREATIVE THINKING FOR WEALTH

The Importance of Innovation in Financial Success

Innovation is often heralded as the cornerstone of progress, and its significance extends deeply into the realm of financial success. At its core, innovation involves the introduction of new ideas, products, or methods that enhance productivity, efficiency, and overall value. This creative process is not merely the domain of technology firms or startups; it is a vital ingredient for any individual or organization aspiring to achieve and sustain wealth.

Understanding Innovation in Financial Context
In the financial sector, innovation can take many forms—from disruptive technologies that redefine industry standards to novel business models that better meet consumer needs. The ability to innovate often distinguishes successful enterprises from those that stagnate. For example, companies that leverage innovative technologies such as artificial intelligence, blockchain, or big data analytics can streamline operations, reduce costs, and enhance customer experiences. This competitive edge not only increases profitability but also opens new revenue streams, thereby contributing to wealth creation.

Innovation as a Driver of Wealth Creation
The relationship between innovation and wealth creation is multifaceted. Firstly, innovation can lead to the development of unique products or services that fulfill unmet needs in the market. When individuals or businesses identify gaps and create solutions,

they position themselves favorably within their respective industries, allowing them to command higher prices and capture greater market share. This ability to innovate translates directly into increased revenues and, ultimately, wealth.

Moreover, innovation fosters a culture of adaptability. In an ever-evolving marketplace, the organizations that thrive are those that embrace change and seek to improve continuously. This adaptability is crucial during times of economic uncertainty or disruption. Businesses that innovate are typically better equipped to pivot their strategies, adjust their offerings, and respond to shifts in consumer behavior, thereby safeguarding their financial success.

Stimulating Innovation: Methods and Practices
To harness the power of innovation for financial success, individuals and organizations must actively foster an environment conducive to creative thinking. Here are several methods to stimulate innovation:

1. Encouraging a Culture of Experimentation: Organizations should promote a culture where experimentation is valued. This includes allowing employees to explore new ideas without the fear of failure. Encouraging creative brainstorming sessions and providing time for employees to work on passion projects can lead to unexpected innovations.

2. Investing in Research and Development: Allocating resources to research and development can yield significant returns. By focusing on understanding market trends and consumer preferences, businesses can create products that resonate with their audience, thus driving sales and profitability.

3. **Leveraging Technology**: In today's digital age, leveraging technology is essential for innovation. Tools such as data analytics can provide insights into consumer behavior, helping businesses tailor their offerings. Automation can streamline operations, allowing more focus on creative processes.

4. **Collaboration and Networking**: Engaging in collaborative efforts with other professionals or organizations can spark new ideas. Networking provides exposure to diverse perspectives and insights that can fuel innovative thinking. Partnerships can also lead to co-creating products that can capture new markets.

Conclusion

In conclusion, innovation is a critical component of financial success. It not only drives the creation of new wealth but also plays a vital role in sustaining that wealth over time. By understanding the importance of innovation and actively cultivating creative environments, individuals and organizations can position themselves to capitalize on opportunities, adapt to changes, and ultimately achieve their financial goals. Embracing innovation is not just a strategy; it is a mindset that can unlock unprecedented pathways to prosperity.

Methods to Stimulate and Expand Creativity

Creativity is not just an innate talent; it can be cultivated through various exercises and practices that enhance imaginative capabilities. In the pursuit of wealth, creative thinking plays a pivotal role in identifying new opportunities, solving problems innovatively, and differentiating oneself in a competitive marketplace. Here, we explore several methods to stimulate and expand creativity that individuals can incorporate into their daily routines.

1. Engage in Brainstorming Sessions
One of the most effective ways to stimulate creativity is through brainstorming. This technique encourages the free flow of ideas without immediate judgment or criticism. To conduct a brainstorming session, set aside a specific time and place where you can focus solely on generating ideas—whether for a business concept, investment strategy, or problem-solving. Write down every idea that comes to mind, no matter how unconventional. After the session, review the list and identify the most promising concepts. This practice not only sparks creativity but also fosters a sense of open-mindedness and exploration.

2. Practice Mind Mapping
Mind mapping is a visual technique that helps organize thoughts and ideas. Start with a central concept, such as a financial goal or business idea, and branch out with related themes, questions, and potential solutions. This spatial representation encourages connections between different concepts and can lead to innovative insights. Mind mapping allows for both linear and non-linear thinking, making it a versatile tool for expanding creative thought.

3. Engage in Diverse Experiences
Exposure to new experiences is crucial for nurturing creativity. Engaging in activities outside your usual routine can provide fresh perspectives and inspiration. This could involve traveling to new places, attending workshops in unrelated fields, or simply trying a new hobby. The key is to step outside your comfort zone and embrace experiences that challenge your existing viewpoints. Interacting with diverse cultures, ideas, and people can enhance

your creative thought process and lead to innovative approaches in financial pursuits.

4. Set Aside Time for Reflection
Creativity often flourishes in moments of solitude and reflection. Designate regular periods for quiet contemplation, whether through meditation, journaling, or simply sitting in silence. Use this time to think deeply about your financial objectives, brainstorm ideas, and reflect on past experiences. Journaling, in particular, can help articulate thoughts and emotions, leading to new insights and creative breakthroughs. Consider asking yourself open-ended questions such as "What if...?" or "How might I approach this differently?" to stimulate imaginative thinking.

5. Incorporate Play into Your Routine
Playfulness can significantly enhance creativity. Engaging in playful activities—be it through games, arts and crafts, or improvisational exercises—facilitates a relaxed mindset conducive to creative thinking. Allowing yourself to experience joy and spontaneity can lead to unexpected ideas and solutions. Activities that encourage collaboration and improvisation, such as group games or team-building exercises, can also foster a creative environment and stimulate collective brainstorming.

6. Limit Constraints and Embrace Flexibility
Creativity thrives when individuals feel free to explore possibilities without constraints. Challenge yourself to think outside the box by imposing fewer restrictions on your ideas. For example, set a goal to generate ten solutions to a problem without considering feasibility initially. This practice encourages expansive thinking, and you may discover viable ideas that would not have surfaced under typical constraints. Embrace flexibility in your approach to

wealth-building, allowing for adjustments and changes that can lead to innovative solutions.

7. Cultivate a Habit of Continuous Learning

Continuous learning is essential for expanding creativity. Stay curious and seek knowledge in various fields, whether through reading, online courses, podcasts, or seminars. The more information and experiences you acquire, the more connections your brain can make, leading to innovative ideas. Surround yourself with intellectually stimulating environments and engage in discussions with others who inspire you.

By incorporating these methods into your daily life, you can enhance your imaginative capabilities, leading to improved creative thinking and ultimately greater financial success. Creativity is a skill that can be developed and refined, providing a valuable asset in your journey to wealth.

Turning Ideas into Profitable Ventures

In the journey to financial success, the ability to transform creative ideas into profitable business ventures is paramount. This process requires not just creativity but also strategic planning, market understanding, and execution. Below are critical steps that can guide aspiring entrepreneurs in this transformation.

1. Validate Your Idea

Before diving into a business venture, it is crucial to validate your idea. This means conducting thorough market research to assess demand for your product or service. Engage potential customers through surveys, interviews, and focus groups to gather insights about their needs and preferences. Understanding the competitive landscape is equally important; analyze existing competitors to identify gaps in the market that your idea can fill. Validation helps you refine your concept and increase the likelihood of success.

2. Develop a Business Plan

Once you've validated your idea, the next step is to create a comprehensive business plan. This document serves as a roadmap for your venture and should include:

- **Executive Summary**: A brief overview of your business concept, goals, and the problem it addresses.
- **Market Analysis**: Detailed insights from your research, including target demographics, market trends, and competitive analysis.
- **Marketing Strategy**: Outline how you will attract and retain customers, including pricing, promotion, and distribution strategies.
- **Operational Plan**: Describe how your business will function daily, including production processes, staffing, and logistics.
- **Financial Projections**: Provide estimates of revenue, expenses, and profit margins for at least the first three years.

A well-structured business plan not only guides your actions but is also essential for attracting investors or securing loans.

3. Create a Minimum Viable Product (MVP)

To minimize risk and investment, develop a Minimum Viable Product (MVP). An MVP is a simplified version of your product that includes only the core features necessary to satisfy early adopters. This allows you to test your concept in the market and gather user feedback without committing significant resources. Based on the responses, iterate and improve the product before a full-scale launch.

4. Build a Brand

Establishing a recognizable brand is vital for attracting customers and differentiating your business from competitors. Develop a unique brand identity that reflects your values and resonates with your target audience. This includes creating a compelling logo, a cohesive color scheme, and a consistent voice across all marketing channels. A strong brand fosters trust and loyalty, which are essential for long-term success.

5. Implement an Effective Marketing Strategy

A robust marketing strategy is crucial for transforming your idea into a profitable venture. Utilize various channels—social media, email marketing, content marketing, and paid advertising—to reach your audience. Tailor your messaging to address the specific needs and interests of your target market. Leverage analytics tools to track the effectiveness of your campaigns and adjust strategies as necessary to optimize results.

6. Establish a Sales Process

Creating a streamlined sales process is essential for converting leads into customers. Define the stages of your sales funnel, from lead generation to closing sales. Train your sales team on effective techniques for engaging potential customers and addressing objections. Providing exceptional customer service throughout the sales process can enhance customer satisfaction and encourage repeat business.

7. Monitor and Adapt

Once your venture is operational, continuously monitor performance metrics to assess success. Regularly collect customer feedback and analyze sales data to identify areas for improvement. The business landscape is ever-changing, and being adaptable is key to sustaining growth and profitability. Regularly revisit your business plan and adjust your strategies based on the insights you gather.

In conclusion, turning ideas into profitable ventures involves a systematic approach that includes validating your concept, developing a solid business plan, creating an MVP, building a strong brand, implementing effective marketing and sales strategies, and remaining adaptable. By following these steps, aspiring entrepreneurs can enhance their chances of transforming their creative concepts into successful and sustainable businesses.

Chapter 7
FORMULATING AN EFFECTIVE ACTION PLAN

Steps to Develop a Realistic Financial Strategy

Creating a realistic financial strategy is a crucial step toward achieving your monetary goals and building wealth. A well-structured financial plan not only provides a roadmap for your financial journey but also helps you navigate challenges and seize opportunities. Here are the essential steps to develop an actionable and achievable financial strategy.

1. Assess Your Current Financial Situation

The first step in developing a financial strategy is to gain a comprehensive understanding of your current financial health. This includes evaluating your income, expenses, assets, liabilities, and net worth. Create a detailed budget that reflects your monthly cash flow, categorizing your income sources and expenditures. This assessment will provide a clear picture of where you stand financially and identify areas that need improvement.

2. Define Your Financial Goals

Once you have a clear understanding of your financial situation, the next step is to define your financial goals. These should be specific, measurable, achievable, relevant, and time-bound (SMART). For example, instead of stating a vague goal like "I want to save money," specify "I want to save $10,000 for a down payment on a house within three years." Clearly articulated goals will help you focus your efforts and measure your progress.

3. Prioritize Your Goals

After establishing your goals, prioritize them based on urgency and importance. Not all financial goals carry the same weight, and it's essential to recognize which ones require immediate attention and which can be pursued over a longer timeframe. For instance, paying off high-interest debt may take precedence over saving for retirement. Prioritization will ensure that you allocate your resources effectively and stay focused on what matters most.

4. Develop an Action Plan

With your goals defined and prioritized, it's time to create an actionable plan. Break down each goal into smaller, manageable steps that outline how you will achieve them. For example, if your goal is to save for a down payment, your action plan might include setting up a dedicated savings account, automating monthly transfers to that account, and cutting unnecessary expenses. This structured approach will make your goals feel more attainable and provide clear direction.

5. Establish a Budget

A budget is a vital tool in your financial strategy. It helps you allocate your income toward your expenses and savings goals systematically. Create a budget that aligns with your action plan, ensuring that you are setting aside enough funds to meet your financial objectives. Revisit and adjust your budget regularly to reflect any changes in income or expenses, keeping your financial strategy dynamic and responsive.

6. Monitor and Adjust Your Strategy

A successful financial strategy requires regular monitoring and adjustments. Periodically review your progress toward your goals, analyzing what is working and what isn't. If you find that you are falling short, reassess your budget, action plan, and even your goals. Life circumstances change, and your financial strategy should be flexible enough to adapt to new challenges and opportunities.

7. Seek Professional Guidance
If you feel overwhelmed or uncertain about your financial strategy, consider seeking professional advice. Financial advisors can provide valuable insights, help refine your goals, and offer tailored strategies based on your individual circumstances. Whether through one-on-one consultations or comprehensive financial planning services, expert guidance can enhance your ability to achieve your financial goals.

Conclusion
Developing a realistic financial strategy is an ongoing process that involves assessing your situation, setting clear goals, creating an actionable plan, and continuously monitoring your progress. By following these steps, you can lay a solid foundation for financial success and navigate your journey toward wealth with confidence and clarity. Remember, the key to a successful financial strategy lies in its adaptability and your commitment to following through.

The Importance of Flexibility in Planning

In the pursuit of wealth, establishing a robust financial plan is essential. However, an equally critical component of successful financial planning is the ability to remain flexible and adaptable. Flexibility in planning allows individuals to navigate the unpredictable nature of life and the economy, ensuring that they can adjust their strategies in response to evolving circumstances.

Responding to Change

The financial landscape is constantly shifting due to various factors, including market fluctuations, changes in personal circumstances, and broader economic conditions. For instance, an unexpected job loss, a global recession, or even personal life events such as marriage or the birth of a child can significantly alter one's financial situation. Those who have rigid plans may find themselves unable to cope with these changes, leading to stress and potential financial setbacks. Conversely, a flexible financial plan allows individuals to reassess their goals, modify their strategies, and pivot when necessary, keeping them on track toward their financial objectives.

Embracing Opportunities

Flexibility is not only about managing adverse changes; it also pertains to recognizing and seizing new opportunities. The world is full of potential wealth-building avenues that can arise unexpectedly, such as investment opportunities, business ventures, or career advancements. A rigid financial plan can blind individuals to these possibilities due to its fixed nature. By maintaining a flexible approach, individuals can adapt their plans to embrace new opportunities that align with their financial goals, thus accelerating their journey to wealth.

Iterative Process of Planning

Financial planning should be viewed as an ongoing, iterative process rather than a one-time event. This perspective encourages individuals to regularly review and assess their plans, making adjustments as necessary based on performance and changing circumstances. For example, if a particular investment is not yielding the expected returns, a flexible planner will reassess their strategy and consider reallocating resources to more promising ventures. This adaptability ensures that individuals remain proactive in their financial management rather than reactive, which can often lead to missed opportunities or increased losses.

Incorporating Feedback

Flexibility also involves the willingness to incorporate feedback and learn from experiences. As individuals progress on their wealth-building journey, they will encounter successes and failures that provide valuable insights into their financial strategies. A flexible planner will take the time to analyze these experiences, learning what works and what doesn't, and adjusting their plans accordingly. This continuous improvement mindset fosters growth and enhances the likelihood of achieving long-term financial success.

The Psychological Aspect of Flexibility

From a psychological standpoint, maintaining flexibility in planning can reduce stress and anxiety. The pressure of adhering to a rigid financial plan can lead to feelings of failure and frustration, especially when circumstances do not align with expectations. Embracing flexibility helps individuals cultivate a more positive outlook, allowing them to view challenges as opportunities for growth rather than insurmountable barriers. This shift in mindset is essential for maintaining motivation and perseverance on the path to wealth.

Conclusion

In conclusion, flexibility in financial planning is paramount for anyone seeking to build wealth. It enables individuals to respond effectively to changing circumstances, embrace new opportunities, engage in an iterative planning process, incorporate valuable feedback, and maintain a healthy psychological outlook. By recognizing the importance of adaptability, individuals can craft financial strategies that not only withstand the test of time but also evolve with them, ultimately leading to greater financial security and prosperity. As the saying goes, "Blessed are the flexible, for they shall not be bent out of shape." Embracing this principle is key to achieving lasting success in the journey toward wealth.

Executing and Monitoring Your Financial Strategy

Once you've formulated a robust financial strategy, the next critical step is execution. This phase involves putting your plans into action while maintaining a keen eye on your progress. Effectively executing and monitoring your financial strategy not only ensures that you stay on track towards achieving your goals but also allows for necessary adjustments along the way.

1. Creating an Actionable Timeline

The first step in executing your financial strategy is to establish a clear and actionable timeline. This timeline should outline when each component of your plan will be executed. Breaking down your goals into smaller, manageable tasks with specific deadlines can significantly enhance your focus and accountability. For instance, if your goal is to save a certain amount each month, set a specific date by which you will automate those savings. This clarity helps in maintaining momentum and reduces the likelihood of procrastination.

2. Establishing Key Performance Indicators (KPIs)

To effectively monitor your progress, you need to establish Key Performance Indicators (KPIs) that align with your financial objectives. KPIs act as measurable benchmarks that provide insight into how well you are executing your plan. For example, if your goal is to increase your investment portfolio by 20% within a year, your

KPIs could include monthly investment growth percentages, portfolio diversification metrics, or the number of new investment opportunities explored each month. Regularly reviewing these indicators allows you to gauge your progress and make informed decisions.

3. Regular Review and Reflection
Setting regular intervals for review is essential in the execution phase. Monthly or quarterly reviews can help you assess whether you are on track to meet your financial objectives. During these reviews, reflect on the following questions:

- Are the strategies I implemented yielding the expected results?
- Have I encountered any obstacles or challenges that need addressing?
- Are my financial goals still aligned with my personal values and lifestyle changes?

This reflective practice enables you to remain adaptable and responsive to changes in your financial landscape.

4. Adjusting Your Strategy as Necessary
Financial markets and personal circumstances can change rapidly, making it vital to remain flexible. If you notice any discrepancies between your projected outcomes and actual results, be prepared to adjust your strategy. This could mean reallocating funds, revising your savings plan, or exploring new investment opportunities. A successful financial strategy is not static; it evolves based on ongoing evaluation and changing circumstances.

5. Accountability Partners

Incorporating an accountability partner can significantly enhance your execution and monitoring efforts. An accountability partner can be a mentor, friend, or financial advisor who shares your financial aspirations and keeps you accountable. Regular check-ins with this partner can ensure that you stay motivated and focused on your goals. They can provide insights, encouragement, and constructive feedback, which can be invaluable as you navigate the financial landscape.

6. Utilizing Financial Tools and Technology

In today's digital age, leveraging technology can streamline the execution and monitoring of your financial strategy. Financial management apps can help track expenses, savings, and investments in real-time. These tools often provide visualizations of your financial journey, making it easier to stay informed about your progress. Automated alerts can notify you of spending thresholds or investment performance changes, ensuring that you remain proactive in managing your financial goals.

Conclusion

Executing and monitoring your financial strategy is an ongoing process that requires diligence, flexibility, and a commitment to continuous improvement. By setting clear timelines, establishing KPIs, conducting regular reviews, and adjusting your strategy as necessary, you can stay on course toward achieving your financial aspirations. Remember, the journey to wealth is not merely about reaching a destination, but rather about fostering a mindset of growth and resilience that propels you forward regardless of the challenges you may encounter.

Chapter 8

MAKING FIRM AND TIMELY DECISIONS

The Impact of Decisiveness on Wealth Accumulation

Decisiveness is a critical trait that can significantly influence wealth accumulation. In the realm of finance, the ability to make timely and informed decisions can set successful individuals apart from those who struggle to achieve their financial aspirations. The relationship between decisiveness and financial success is rooted in several key factors: opportunity recognition, risk management, and the momentum created through decisive action.

Opportunity Recognition
In a rapidly changing economic landscape, opportunities for wealth generation often present themselves unexpectedly. Being decisive allows individuals to recognize and seize these opportunities before they vanish. For instance, an investor who can quickly assess and act on a promising stock or real estate deal usually benefits from a first-mover advantage. Conversely, indecision can result in missed opportunities, as others may capitalize on what was once a potential financial windfall. This is particularly evident in fast-paced markets where trends can shift overnight. Those who hesitate may find that the window of opportunity has closed, leaving them at a disadvantage.

Risk Management
Decisiveness is also fundamental to effective risk management. Financial ventures inherently involve uncertainty, and the ability to make quick yet informed decisions can mitigate potential losses. For example, an entrepreneur faced with a market downturn must

decide whether to pivot their business strategy or double down on their current approach. A decisive leader can analyze the situation, weigh the risks, and choose a course of action that minimizes potential fallout. This proactive approach not only aids in protecting current assets but also positions individuals to recover swiftly from setbacks. In contrast, those who remain indecisive may prolong a crisis, exacerbating losses and diminishing their wealth-building potential.

Momentum Creation
The act of making decisions also generates momentum, a crucial element for financial success. When individuals take decisive steps toward their goals, it creates a ripple effect that can lead to further opportunities and achievements. This momentum fosters a sense of progress and motivation, encouraging individuals to continue making informed financial choices. For example, a person who decides to invest in a new venture may feel empowered to explore additional avenues for growth, such as diversifying their investment portfolio or starting a side business. This cumulative effect is vital, as the wealth-building process is often not linear; it requires ongoing effort and adaptability.

Enhancing Decision-Making Abilities
Developing the ability to make effective decisions is essential for anyone looking to accumulate wealth. This involves cultivating analytical skills, emotional intelligence, and a strong understanding of personal financial goals. Techniques such as setting clear criteria for decision-making, practicing mindfulness to reduce emotional biases, and learning from past experiences can significantly enhance one's decisiveness. Moreover, creating a habit of reflecting on decisions—both successful and unsuccessful—can provide

valuable insights that inform future choices, leading to a more agile and effective decision-making process.

Conclusion

In conclusion, the impact of decisiveness on wealth accumulation cannot be overstated. Timely decisions allow individuals to recognize and act upon opportunities, effectively manage risks, and create momentum that propels them toward financial success. By honing their decision-making abilities and fostering a decisive mindset, individuals can enhance their financial outcomes and navigate the complexities of wealth building with greater confidence. Ultimately, the path to prosperity is paved with decisive actions that align with one's financial goals and values, transforming aspirations into tangible results.

Enhancing Decision-Making Abilities

Effective decision-making is a cornerstone of financial success. The ability to make informed, timely, and confident decisions can differentiate between seizing opportunities and missing out. Here are several techniques to enhance your decision-making abilities, especially in the realm of personal finance and wealth building.

1. Gather Relevant Information

Before making any significant financial decision, it is essential to gather all relevant information. This involves conducting thorough research on the matter at hand. Whether considering an investment, purchasing a property, or launching a business venture, understanding the market, potential risks, and benefits is crucial. Utilize reputable sources such as financial news, industry reports, and expert analyses. The more informed you are, the better equipped you will be to make sound decisions.

2. Define Clear Objectives

Having clear financial objectives serves as a guiding framework for your decision-making process. Define what you want to achieve—whether it's saving for retirement, buying a home, or funding your children's education. Specific goals create a roadmap, enabling you to evaluate decisions based on how well they align with your objectives. When faced with choices, ask yourself: "Does this decision bring me closer to my financial goals?"

3. Analyze Pros and Cons

A systematic approach to decision-making involves analyzing the pros and cons of each option. Create a list or a matrix that outlines the advantages and disadvantages associated with a particular choice. This visual representation can help clarify the potential outcomes and assist in weighing the risks against the rewards. Understanding the trade-offs involved will empower you to make a more balanced and rational decision.

4. Consult Trusted Advisors

Sometimes, seeking the opinion of others can provide valuable insights. Consult with trusted financial advisors, mentors, or peers who have experience in the area you are exploring. They can offer perspectives that you may not have considered and help you avoid common pitfalls. Be open to constructive criticism and use it to refine your decision-making process.

5. Embrace a Decision-Making Framework

Implementing a structured decision-making framework can enhance your ability to evaluate options consistently. One effective model is the "DECIDE" framework:
- Define the problem.
- Explore the alternatives.

- Consider the consequences.
- Identify your values.
- Decide and take action.
- Evaluate the decision's effectiveness.

By following this framework, you can systematically approach decisions, ensuring that you consider all relevant factors before committing to a course of action.

6. Practice Mindfulness and Emotional Regulation
Emotions can heavily influence decision-making, often leading to impulsive or irrational choices. Practicing mindfulness can help you become more aware of your emotional state and how it affects your decisions. Techniques such as meditation, deep breathing exercises, or journaling can improve emotional regulation, allowing you to approach financial decisions with a clear mind and a rational perspective.

7. Learn from Past Decisions
Reflecting on past decisions—both successful and unsuccessful—can provide valuable learning experiences. Take time to analyze what worked, what didn't, and why. This reflection can help you recognize patterns in your decision-making and avoid repeating past mistakes. Documenting your financial decisions and their outcomes can serve as a reference for future choices.

8. Set a Time Limit for Decisions
Procrastination can be a significant barrier to effective decision-making. Set a time limit for making choices, especially for those that are time-sensitive. This encourages you to focus and streamline your thought process, reducing the tendency to overthink and become paralyzed by indecision.

By implementing these techniques, you can enhance your decision-making abilities, leading to more effective financial choices and ultimately greater success in your wealth-building journey. Remember, effective decision-making is not just about making the right choice; it's about making informed choices that align with your financial goals and values.

Learning from Past Decisions

One of the most powerful tools for achieving financial success is the ability to learn from past decisions. This process involves reflecting on previous experiences—both positive and negative—to extract valuable insights that can guide future financial strategies. By analyzing past choices, individuals can identify patterns, understand their decision-making processes, and refine their approaches to wealth accumulation.

1. The Importance of Reflection

Reflection is the cornerstone of learning from past decisions. It requires individuals to take a step back and assess the outcomes of their financial choices. This process can involve reviewing investment decisions, spending habits, and the overall effectiveness of financial strategies. Successful individuals often maintain a journal or log where they document their decisions, the rationale behind them, and the outcomes. This practice not only fosters accountability but also provides a tangible record to reference when making future choices.

2. Identifying Patterns and Trends

When analyzing past decisions, it is essential to look for patterns and trends. For example, an individual may notice that their investments in certain sectors consistently yield positive returns while others result in losses. Recognizing such patterns can help refine investment strategies and inform future decisions. Furthermore, individuals can analyze their response to market fluctuations, economic conditions, or personal financial crises to better prepare for similar situations in the future.

3. Understanding Emotional Influences
Emotions play a significant role in decision-making. Many financial decisions are influenced by fear, greed, or overconfidence. By reflecting on past decisions, individuals can identify instances where emotions may have clouded their judgment. For example, an impulsive purchase driven by a fear of missing out (FOMO) could lead to regret if it resulted in financial strain. Understanding these emotional triggers allows individuals to develop strategies to mitigate their impact, such as setting strict investment guidelines or creating a cooling-off period for major purchases.

4. Evaluating Decision-Making Processes
Beyond the outcomes, it is vital to assess the decision-making process itself. This includes examining the factors that influenced the decisions, such as available information, peer advice, or market research. Understanding which sources of information were reliable and which were misleading can enhance future financial strategies. Individuals can also evaluate whether their decision-making process was systematic and analytical or impulsive and reactive. By identifying strengths and weaknesses in their approach, they can cultivate a more disciplined and informed strategy moving forward.

5. Learning from Mistakes and Successes
Both successes and failures offer critical lessons. A successful investment can reveal the importance of doing thorough research

and timing. Conversely, a failed venture can highlight the need for risk assessment and diversification. It is crucial to embrace failures as learning opportunities rather than sources of discouragement. Adopting a growth mindset—viewing challenges as chances to learn—can foster resilience and improve long-term financial decision-making.

6. Implementing Lessons in Future Strategies
Finally, the insights gained from past decisions must be actively implemented in future strategies. This can involve setting specific guidelines based on previous experiences, such as investing only in sectors where one has demonstrated success or adhering to a predetermined risk level. Additionally, individuals can create contingency plans based on past mistakes, ensuring they are better prepared for unforeseen circumstances.

In conclusion, learning from past decisions is a vital step in the journey toward financial success. By engaging in reflective practices, identifying patterns, understanding emotional influences, evaluating decision-making processes, embracing both successes and failures, and implementing lessons learned, individuals can craft more effective financial strategies that pave the way for sustainable wealth accumulation. The ability to analyze and adapt based on past experiences not only enhances decision-making skills but also builds the confidence necessary to navigate the complexities of financial management.

Chapter 9

BUILDING STEADFAST DETERMINATION

The Role of Persistence in Achieving Wealth

Persistence is often cited as one of the most critical attributes of successful individuals, particularly in the pursuit of wealth. While skills, knowledge, and strategies are undeniably important, it is persistence—the unwavering commitment to continue striving toward one's goals despite obstacles—that often distinguishes the wealthy from those who falter along their journey.

The path to financial success is seldom linear; it is typically fraught with challenges, setbacks, and periods of uncertainty. During these times, the ability to maintain focus and continue working toward one's objectives becomes paramount. This is where persistence plays a crucial role. Persistence is the steadfastness to keep pushing forward, to continue taking action even when circumstances are not favorable. It is this unwavering determination that enables individuals to overcome adversity and stay the course.

Understanding the Nature of Persistence

At its core, persistence is about more than just hard work; it is about cultivating a mindset that embraces challenges and views setbacks as opportunities for growth. For many successful entrepreneurs and investors, the journey to wealth is marked by failures and missteps that could have easily derailed their ambitions. However, those who persist are the ones who learn from their experiences, adapt their strategies, and continue moving forward. This resilience not only enhances an individual's ability to achieve financial goals but also fosters personal growth and development.

The Connection Between Persistence and Wealth Building
Research has shown that persistence is a key predictor of long-term success in various fields, including business and finance. For example, many successful entrepreneurs share stories of initial failures before achieving significant financial milestones. They often highlight how their willingness to keep trying, to refine their ideas, and to learn from failures ultimately led to their eventual success. This connection between persistence and wealth-building is not merely anecdotal; it reflects a broader truth about the importance of resilience in the face of challenges.

In financial contexts, persistent individuals are more likely to remain committed to their investment strategies, resist panic selling during market downturns, and continue seeking out new opportunities even after experiencing losses. This long-term perspective allows them to benefit from compounding returns, which can lead to substantial wealth accumulation over time.

Strategies to Cultivate Persistence

1. Set Clear Goals: Having a well-defined financial goal provides direction and motivation. When individuals know what they are working toward, they are more likely to stay committed, even when faced with challenges.

2. Embrace a Growth Mindset: Understanding that skills and intelligence can be developed through effort and learning fosters a mindset that is conducive to persistence. Adopting this perspective can help individuals view setbacks as integral to their growth rather than as insurmountable obstacles.

3. Develop a Support Network: Surrounding oneself with like-minded individuals who encourage and motivate can bolster persistence. A supportive community can provide the necessary encouragement to keep pushing forward, especially during tough times.

4. Practice Self-Reflection: Regularly reflecting on one's progress, challenges faced, and lessons learned can reinforce the importance of persistence. Acknowledging achievements, no matter how small, can help maintain motivation.

5. Celebrate Small Wins: Recognizing and celebrating incremental successes can help sustain momentum. Each small victory serves as a reminder of progress made and reinforces the commitment to continue.

Conclusion

In conclusion, persistence is a fundamental component of achieving wealth. It empowers individuals to navigate the inevitable ups and downs of their financial journeys, fostering resilience and adaptability. By embracing persistence, setting clear goals, and cultivating a supportive environment, aspiring wealth builders can enhance their likelihood of success. Financial prosperity is rarely a result of a single effort; rather, it is the cumulative effect of relentless determination, adaptive strategies, and an unwavering commitment to one's vision.

Overcoming Challenges and Staying Motivated

Wealth-building is often portrayed as a linear path to success, yet the reality is fraught with challenges and setbacks that can derail even the most determined individuals. To thrive in the pursuit of financial success, one must cultivate resilience and maintain motivation, especially in the face of obstacles. Here, we will explore effective strategies to overcome challenges and foster sustained motivation during your wealth-building journey.

1. Embrace a Growth Mindset

At the heart of overcoming challenges lies the concept of a growth mindset, a term popularized by psychologist Carol Dweck. Individuals with a growth mindset view challenges as opportunities for growth rather than insurmountable barriers. By reframing setbacks as learning experiences, you can develop resilience and remain motivated. Acknowledge that failures are not the end, but stepping stones to success. When faced with a challenge, ask yourself, "What can I learn from this experience?" This mindset shift can empower you to persist in your efforts, adapting your strategies as needed.

2. Set Incremental Goals

While having a vision for wealth is vital, breaking that vision into smaller, achievable goals can make the journey less daunting. Each time you achieve a small goal, you create a sense of accomplishment that fuels your motivation. For instance, rather than aiming solely to save a significant amount of money, set monthly or quarterly savings targets. Celebrate these milestones, no matter how minor they may seem. Each success adds to your motivation and reinforces your commitment to the larger objective.

3. Develop a Support System

Surrounding yourself with like-minded individuals who share your financial aspirations can provide invaluable support. A strong network can offer encouragement, accountability, and new perspectives on overcoming challenges. Engage in communities—whether in-person or online—where discussions about wealth-building are encouraged. Share your struggles and learn from others' experiences. This collective energy can help keep you motivated and inspired, particularly during tough times.

4. Practice Self-Compassion

As you navigate the ups and downs of your wealth-building journey, it's essential to practice self-compassion. Recognize that everyone encounters obstacles, and being hard on yourself for setbacks can diminish motivation. Instead, treat yourself with kindness and understanding. When challenges arise, remind yourself that it's okay to feel frustrated or disheartened. Acknowledge your emotions without judgment and focus on constructive actions you can take moving forward.

5. Visualize Success

Visualization is a powerful tool that can enhance motivation. Take time to vividly imagine your financial goals and the life you envision. Create a vision board or write down your goals and aspirations, making them tangible. By regularly visualizing your success, you reinforce your commitment to your objectives. This practice can serve as a constant reminder of why you started your journey, helping you stay focused and motivated when faced with challenges.

6. Reassess and Adjust Your Strategies

Challenges often highlight the need for flexibility in your approach to wealth-building. If you encounter an obstacle, take a step back and reassess your strategies. Are they still aligned with your goals? Sometimes, a small adjustment can lead to significant breakthroughs. Being adaptable allows you to pivot when necessary, maintaining momentum toward your financial aspirations.

7. Maintain a Positive Environment

Your environment plays a crucial role in your motivation levels. Surround yourself with positivity—be it through uplifting literature, motivational podcasts, or inspiring individuals. Limit exposure to negativity, whether from pessimistic people or discouraging media. A positive environment nurtures resilience and keeps you focused on your financial journey.

In conclusion, overcoming challenges and maintaining motivation in the wealth-building journey requires a multifaceted approach. By embracing a growth mindset, setting incremental goals, fostering a supportive network, practicing self-compassion, visualizing success, reassessing strategies, and cultivating a positive environment, you can navigate obstacles with resilience and keep your motivation alive. Remember, wealth is not just about financial accumulation; it's about the personal growth and lessons learned along the way.

Developing Resilience Through Continuous Effort

Resilience is the cornerstone of achieving financial success. It is the ability to withstand adversity, adapt to challenges, and emerge stronger from setbacks. For anyone on the journey to wealth, developing resilience through continuous effort is crucial. This section delves into the significance of persistence, the mechanisms that foster resilience, and actionable strategies to cultivate this vital trait.

Understanding Resilience

Resilience is not merely about bouncing back from failure; it is about learning and growing from those experiences. In the financial realm, setbacks are inevitable. Market fluctuations, failed investments, and unforeseen expenses can throw even the most meticulously planned strategies off course. The ability to navigate these challenges with a positive attitude and a commitment to keep moving forward is what ultimately differentiates successful individuals from those who falter.

The Role of Continuous Effort

Continuous effort is integral to building resilience. It involves consistently pushing forward, even when the path is fraught with obstacles. This dedication fosters a mindset that views challenges as opportunities for growth rather than insurmountable barriers. Each effort, whether successful or not, contributes to a deeper understanding of the financial landscape and enhances one's capacity to make informed decisions in the future.

Strategies for Developing Resilience

1. Embrace a Growth Mindset: Cultivating a growth mindset is pivotal for resilience. This involves recognizing that abilities and intelligence can be developed through dedication and hard work. When faced with setbacks, individuals with a growth mindset are more likely to seek solutions and learn from their experiences rather than succumb to despair. Adopting this perspective can transform challenges into valuable learning experiences, laying the groundwork for future success.

2. Set Realistic Goals: While striving for wealth, it is essential to set achievable goals. Unrealistic expectations can lead to frustration and disappointment, making it difficult to persist in the face of challenges. By establishing clear, manageable objectives, individuals can experience small victories that bolster their confidence and reinforce their commitment to their financial journey.

3. Develop a Support System: Surrounding oneself with supportive individuals can significantly enhance resilience. A network of mentors, peers, and like-minded individuals offers encouragement, shares insights, and provides accountability. Engaging with this network during challenging times can serve as a reminder that setbacks are a normal part of the journey, and shared experiences can foster a sense of camaraderie and collective resilience.

4. Practice Mindfulness and Stress Management: Resilience is closely tied to emotional well-being. Practicing mindfulness techniques, such as meditation or deep-breathing exercises, can help individuals manage stress and maintain focus in the face of adversity. By cultivating emotional regulation, individuals can approach financial challenges with a clear mind, allowing them to make thoughtful decisions rather than impulsive reactions driven by stress.

5. Reflect and Adapt: Continuous effort involves a cycle of reflection and adaptation. After encountering a setback, it is crucial to assess what went wrong and why. This reflective practice allows individuals to glean insights from their experiences, enabling them to adjust their strategies moving forward. By viewing setbacks as opportunities for learning, individuals can develop a more resilient approach to their financial endeavors.

6. Celebrate Progress: Acknowledging progress, no matter how small, is vital for maintaining motivation. Celebrating milestones reinforces a sense of achievement and encourages individuals to continue putting in the effort. This practice fosters a positive mindset and encourages persistence, even when larger goals may seem distant.

Conclusion
Developing resilience through continuous effort is essential for anyone aspiring to achieve financial success. By embracing a growth mindset, setting realistic goals, cultivating supportive relationships, managing stress, reflecting on experiences, and celebrating progress, individuals can build the resilience necessary to navigate the inevitable ups and downs of the wealth-building journey. In doing so, they not only enhance their capacity to overcome challenges but also lay a solid foundation for lasting success.

Chapter 10

CREATING A NETWORK OF SUCCESS PARTNERS

The Value of a Supportive Professional Network

In the journey towards financial prosperity, one of the most pivotal yet often overlooked factors is the role of a supportive professional network. The adage "it's not what you know, but who you know" resonates deeply within the context of wealth accumulation. Relationships can significantly impact access to opportunities, resources, and knowledge, ultimately shaping an individual's financial destiny.

Building Relationships: The Foundation of Networking

At its core, networking is about building and nurturing relationships with individuals who share similar interests, goals, or expertise. A supportive professional network can provide a safety net of encouragement, guidance, and opportunities. Relationships fostered in this way can lead to mentorship, collaborations, and partnerships that may otherwise be unattainable. For instance, a mentor can offer invaluable insights drawn from their own experiences, helping you navigate challenges and avoid common pitfalls. Their guidance can expedite your learning curve and enhance your decision-making abilities.

Access to Opportunities

One of the most immediate benefits of a robust professional network is access to exclusive opportunities. Many lucrative job openings, investment prospects, and collaborative ventures are often shared within networks before they are publicly advertised. Individuals who actively engage with their networks are more likely to receive referrals and recommendations, which can be critical in competitive environments. Furthermore, relationships can lead to introductions to influential individuals in various industries, opening doors that were previously closed.

Leveraging Collective Knowledge
A supportive network acts as a repository of collective knowledge. Each member brings unique experiences, skills, and perspectives, contributing to a wealth of information that can be tapped into. Engaging with diverse professionals can broaden your understanding of different markets, industries, and practices. By sharing insights and best practices, network members can help each other identify trends, anticipate challenges, and devise innovative solutions. This collaborative environment fosters a culture of learning and growth, essential for financial advancement.

Emotional Support and Accountability
Beyond tangible benefits, the emotional support derived from a professional network can be transformative. The path to financial success is often fraught with challenges and setbacks. Having a supportive network provides a sense of belonging and reassurance during difficult times. Members can celebrate each other's achievements, offer encouragement during failures, and remind one another of their goals and aspirations. This emotional reinforcement is crucial for maintaining motivation and resilience, both of which are essential for long-term success.

Moreover, a network can serve as an accountability group. Sharing your financial goals with trusted individuals encourages commitment and follow-through. When you know that others are invested in your success, you are more likely to stay focused and disciplined in your efforts.

Strategies for Building Your Network
To harness the value of a supportive professional network, intentional effort is required. Start by identifying individuals within your existing circles who align with your financial aspirations. Attend industry conferences, workshops, and networking events to meet new contacts. Online platforms such as LinkedIn can also be instrumental in expanding your professional connections.

Engage actively with your network by participating in discussions, sharing valuable content, and offering assistance where possible. Building a reputation as a helpful and knowledgeable individual will encourage others to reciprocate, strengthening the bonds within your network.

Conclusion
In summary, a supportive professional network is an invaluable asset in the pursuit of financial success. Not only does it provide access to opportunities and knowledge, but it also fosters emotional support and accountability. By investing time and effort in cultivating meaningful relationships, you can significantly enhance your financial journey, turning aspirations into reality. The relationships you build today lay the groundwork for the wealth you can create tomorrow.

Connecting with Like-Minded Individuals
In the pursuit of wealth and financial success, the importance of surrounding oneself with like-minded individuals cannot be overstated. Building a supportive network of peers who share similar aspirations and values can significantly enhance your

journey towards prosperity. This section delves into effective approaches for connecting with such individuals, which can foster collaboration, motivation, and opportunities for mutual growth.

1. Identify Your Goals and Values
Before seeking out like-minded individuals, it is essential to clarify your own financial goals and personal values. Understanding what you want to achieve and why it matters to you lays a solid foundation for meaningful connections. Reflect on your aspirations, whether they involve entrepreneurship, investment, or career advancement, and articulate your core values, such as integrity, innovation, or service. This self-awareness will guide you in identifying individuals who resonate with your vision.

2. Leverage Social Media and Online Communities
In today's digital age, social media platforms and online communities provide unprecedented access to networks of like-minded individuals. Platforms like LinkedIn, Facebook groups, and online forums dedicated to finance and entrepreneurship can serve as powerful tools for connection. Engage actively in discussions, share your insights, and contribute value to these communities. By showcasing your knowledge and enthusiasm, you can attract individuals who share your interests and goals.

3. Attend Networking Events and Workshops
Participating in networking events, seminars, and workshops related to financial growth is a proactive way to meet like-minded individuals. Look for local meetups, conferences, or industry-specific events where you can connect with others who are also focused on wealth-building. These gatherings provide fertile ground for establishing relationships, exchanging ideas, and exploring potential collaborations. Approach conversations with

genuine curiosity and open-mindedness to foster deeper connections.

4. Join Professional Organizations and Clubs
Professional organizations often gather individuals with shared goals and interests. Joining such groups can provide a structured environment to network with others committed to financial success. Look for organizations in your field or those focused on personal finance, entrepreneurship, or investment. Actively participate in their activities, attend meetings, and offer your expertise where possible. This involvement not only expands your network but also positions you as a valuable member of the community.

5. Seek Out Mentorship Opportunities
Connecting with mentors who have successfully navigated the path to wealth can be immensely beneficial. Mentors provide guidance, share their experiences, and can introduce you to their network of like-minded individuals. Seek out mentors through professional organizations, networking events, or even social media. Be open to learning from their journey and leverage their insights to enhance your own financial strategies.

6. Engage in Collaborative Projects
One of the most effective ways to build relationships with like-minded individuals is through collaboration. Identify projects or initiatives within your network that align with your goals and values. Working together on a common objective not only strengthens relationships but also fosters a sense of accountability and shared purpose. Whether it's co-authoring a blog, launching a startup, or organizing a community event, collaborative efforts can lead to valuable connections.

7. Follow Up and Nurture Relationships

After making initial connections, it's vital to nurture these relationships over time. Follow up with individuals you meet, express your appreciation for their insights, and keep the lines of communication open. Use social media to stay in touch, share relevant articles, and engage with their content. By maintaining these connections, you create a supportive network that can provide encouragement, advice, and opportunities as you pursue your wealth-building journey.

In conclusion, connecting with like-minded individuals is a critical step in achieving financial success. By being intentional about your networking efforts, you can create a powerful support system that not only motivates you but also opens doors to new opportunities. Embrace the journey of building these relationships, and watch as your aspirations align with a community of individuals equally dedicated to the pursuit of prosperity.

Collaborating for Mutual Financial Advancement

In the quest for financial success, the age-old adage "two heads are better than one" rings particularly true. Collaboration is not merely a strategic advantage; it is often a necessity in today's interconnected economic landscape. By leveraging partnerships and collaborations, individuals and businesses can create a synergistic effect that enhances their potential for wealth creation. This section explores the critical aspects of collaboration for mutual financial advancement, emphasizing the benefits, strategies, and best practices that can facilitate successful partnerships.

The Power of Collaborative Synergy

At its core, collaboration is about pooling resources, knowledge, and networks to achieve common financial goals. When individuals or organizations come together, they can combine their unique strengths, leading to innovative solutions and increased productivity. For instance, two entrepreneurs might collaborate on a project where one brings technical expertise while the other contributes marketing acumen. This partnership not only broadens their capabilities but also minimizes risks associated with financial ventures.

Additionally, collaboration fosters creative problem-solving. In times of economic uncertainty, pooling ideas and resources can result in innovative approaches that might not emerge in isolation. Diverse perspectives challenge conventional thinking, enabling partners to navigate obstacles more effectively and capitalize on emerging opportunities.

Identifying Potential Partners

The first step in fostering successful collaborations is identifying potential partners whose goals align with your own. This process involves assessing individual strengths, weaknesses, and values to ensure compatibility. Ideal partners should complement your skills and add value to your financial objectives.

Networking is crucial in this regard. Attend industry events, join professional organizations, and engage on social media platforms to connect with like-minded individuals. Be open to collaborations that might not seem immediately beneficial but could lead to unexpected opportunities. Relationships built on trust and mutual respect are more likely to yield fruitful partnerships.

Establishing Clear Goals and Expectations

Once potential partners are identified, it's essential to establish clear goals and expectations. Open communication is vital to ensure that all parties are aligned in terms of objectives, roles, and responsibilities. This clarity helps prevent misunderstandings and ensures that everyone is working towards a shared vision.

Consider drafting a collaboration agreement that outlines each partner's contributions, profit-sharing arrangements, and exit strategies. This formal documentation not only provides legal protection but also reinforces commitment to the partnership.

Leveraging Resources and Skills

Collaboration allows partners to leverage each other's resources and skills effectively. This could mean sharing financial investments, accessing each other's customer bases, or utilizing complementary technologies. For example, a small business might collaborate with a larger firm to gain access to advanced marketing tools and strategies, enhancing its reach and visibility in the market.

Moreover, partnerships can facilitate knowledge sharing, allowing each party to learn from the other's experiences and expertise. This continuous exchange of information can lead to improved decision-making and enhanced competitive advantage.

Monitoring Progress and Adapting Strategies

Successful collaborations require ongoing evaluation and adaptation. Regularly assess the partnership's progress towards shared goals and be willing to make adjustments as necessary. This could involve refining strategies, reallocating resources, or even dissolving the partnership if it no longer serves mutual interests.

Effective collaboration is a dynamic process that requires commitment, flexibility, and a willingness to evolve. By maintaining open lines of communication and fostering a culture of feedback, partners can navigate challenges and celebrate successes together.

Conclusion

In conclusion, collaboration for mutual financial advancement is a powerful strategy that can significantly enhance an individual's or organization's wealth-building efforts. By identifying compatible partners, establishing clear goals, leveraging shared resources, and continuously monitoring progress, individuals can create synergies that lead to shared success. Embracing collaboration not only fosters innovation and creativity but also builds a supportive network that can propel all parties towards greater financial achievements. In a world where the ability to adapt and collaborate is increasingly important, harnessing the power of partnership may well be the key to unlocking long-term prosperity.

Chapter 11

CHANNELING PERSONAL ENERGY INTO SUCCESS

Understanding Energy's Impact on Productivity

In the pursuit of financial success, one often overlooks the pivotal role that personal energy plays in productivity. Energy, in this context, refers not only to physical stamina but also to mental and emotional vigor. The interplay between these forms of energy significantly influences our effectiveness in achieving financial goals. Understanding this relationship can empower individuals to optimize their work habits and enhance overall productivity.

The Relationship Between Energy Levels and Productivity
At its core, productivity is about achieving maximum output with the least amount of input. Energy levels directly affect our ability to focus, engage, and innovate. When energy is high, individuals tend to approach tasks with enthusiasm, creativity, and resilience. Conversely, low energy can lead to lethargy, decreased motivation, and an inability to concentrate, ultimately stalling progress toward financial objectives.

Research has shown that our bodies operate on circadian rhythms, which dictate energy fluctuations throughout the day. Recognizing these natural cycles can help individuals schedule their most demanding tasks during periods of peak energy. For instance, many people experience heightened alertness in the mid-morning; capitalizing on this time for critical decision-making or strategic planning can lead to superior outcomes.

Directing Energy Toward Financial Goals

To maximize productivity, it is essential to direct energy toward specific financial goals. This can be achieved through several strategies:

1. Prioritizing Tasks: Identifying and prioritizing tasks that align with financial objectives ensures that energy is expended on activities that yield the highest returns. Utilizing tools like the Eisenhower Matrix can help distinguish between urgent and important tasks, guiding individuals to focus their energy where it is most needed.

2. Creating a Conducive Environment: The workspace significantly impacts energy levels. A well-organized, inspiring environment can uplift mood and productivity. Elements such as natural light, ergonomic furniture, and minimal distractions can enhance focus and energize individuals to work more effectively.

3. Incorporating Breaks: Continuous work without breaks can lead to burnout and diminished energy. Implementing regular breaks—such as the Pomodoro Technique—can sustain energy levels throughout the day. Short breaks allow the mind to reset and can enhance creativity and problem-solving abilities when returning to tasks.

4. Maintaining Physical Health: Physical health is intrinsically linked to energy levels. Regular exercise, a balanced diet, and adequate sleep are crucial for maintaining high energy. Engaging in physical activity increases blood flow and oxygen to the brain, enhancing cognitive function and overall productivity.

5. Practicing Mindfulness and Stress Management: Emotional and mental energy is just as critical as physical energy. Techniques such as meditation, deep breathing, and mindfulness can help manage stress and foster a positive outlook. A calm, centered mind is more productive and capable of navigating the challenges associated with wealth-building.

Sustaining Energy for Long-Term Success
Sustaining high energy levels over the long term requires commitment to self-care and a proactive approach to managing one's workload. It is vital to regularly assess energy levels and adjust routines accordingly. Adopting a growth mindset encourages individuals to view challenges as opportunities for development rather than threats, fostering resilience and sustained motivation.

In conclusion, understanding the impact of energy on productivity is essential for anyone aiming to build wealth. By recognizing energy patterns, directing energy toward meaningful financial goals, and maintaining overall well-being, individuals can enhance their productivity. This, in turn, paves the way for greater financial success and fulfillment. The journey to prosperity is not solely about hard work but also about harnessing and sustaining the energy that drives effective work habits.

Directing Energy Towards Financial Goals

In the quest for financial success, energy management stands as a pivotal factor that influences productivity and outcomes. The ability to harness and direct personal energy towards productive activities can differentiate between stagnation and progress in wealth accumulation. Here, we explore effective methods to focus your energy on achieving financial goals.

1. Establishing Clear Priorities

The first step in directing energy towards financial goals is to establish clear priorities. Begin by identifying your top financial objectives, whether they involve saving a specific amount, investing in a business, or reducing debt. By categorizing these goals based on urgency and importance, you can allocate your energy accordingly. Implementing the Eisenhower Matrix, which divides tasks into four quadrants based on urgency and importance, can assist in visualizing which financial activities require immediate attention and which can be scheduled for later.

2. Creating a Structured Routine

Once priorities are set, developing a structured routine is essential. A well-defined daily or weekly schedule allows you to allocate dedicated time blocks specifically for financial activities. This could include activities such as budgeting, researching investment opportunities, or networking with potential partners. By systematically integrating these tasks into your routine, you cultivate a habit of productivity, ensuring that your energy is consistently directed toward financial growth.

3. Setting Specific Time Limits

While structure is key, so is the management of time spent on each activity. Setting specific time limits for financial tasks can enhance focus and prevent burnout. For instance, allocate a fixed duration to analyze market trends or to work on a business plan. This approach helps to maintain intensity and concentration, ensuring that energy is utilized efficiently without leading to fatigue. The Pomodoro Technique, which involves working for 25 minutes followed by a 5-minute break, can be a helpful method to sustain energy levels while promoting productivity.

4. Engaging in Energy-Boosting Activities

Physical and mental well-being profoundly impacts your energy levels. Engaging in regular physical exercise, maintaining a balanced diet, and ensuring adequate sleep are critical components of sustaining high energy levels. Activities such as yoga or meditation can also enhance mental clarity and reduce stress, allowing for a more focused approach to financial tasks. When your body and mind are in optimal condition, your ability to direct energy towards productive financial activities improves significantly.

5. Harnessing the Power of Visualization

Visualization techniques can be a powerful method to direct energy towards your financial goals. By vividly imagining the successful attainment of your financial objectives, you create a mental picture that energizes your pursuits. Spend a few moments each day visualizing your financial success: whether it's the feeling of financial freedom, the joy of achieving a savings milestone, or the satisfaction of a successful investment. This practice not only boosts motivation but also aligns your subconscious to work towards these goals, enhancing your overall focus and energy.

6. Surrounding Yourself with Positive Influences

The people you interact with can significantly influence your energy levels and motivation. Surrounding yourself with positive, like-minded individuals who share similar financial aspirations can create an energizing environment. Engage in discussions that inspire and motivate you, and seek accountability partners who can support your financial journey. This community can provide encouragement, facilitate networking opportunities, and help you stay focused on your goals.

7. Periodic Reflection and Adjustment

Finally, it is crucial to periodically reflect on your progress and adjust your strategies accordingly. Regularly assess whether the methods you are using to direct your energy toward financial goals are effective. If certain practices are not yielding the desired results, be flexible and willing to modify your approach. This adaptability ensures that your energy remains directed towards the most impactful financial activities.

In conclusion, directing energy towards financial goals is a multifaceted process that involves prioritization, structure, well-being, visualization, positive influences, and reflection. By implementing these methods, you not only enhance your productivity but also create a powerful momentum that propels you forward on your journey to wealth. Through conscious and focused energy management, you can transform aspirations into tangible financial achievements.

Sustaining Energy for Long-Term Success

Achieving long-term financial objectives requires not just ambition and strategy but also sustained energy and resilience. Energy is the vital force that propels individuals toward their goals, influencing productivity, creativity, and overall well-being. Here are several tips for sustaining energy to remain focused on long-term financial success.

1. Establish a Balanced Routine

Creating a balanced daily routine is crucial for maintaining energy levels over the long term. This includes establishing a consistent sleep schedule, engaging in regular physical activity, and ensuring proper nutrition. Sleep is vital for cognitive function and emotional regulation, while exercise boosts mood and energy through the release of endorphins. A diet rich in nutrients supports brain health and stamina, providing the necessary fuel for sustained productivity. Incorporating breaks into your daily schedule can also help recharge your mental batteries, allowing for more effective work intervals.

2. Set Realistic Milestones
Long-term financial goals can often feel overwhelming. Breaking these goals down into smaller, manageable milestones can help maintain motivation and energy levels. By celebrating these small accomplishments, you reinforce positive behavior and create a sense of progression. This incremental approach also allows for regular assessment of strategies, ensuring that you remain aligned with your ultimate financial objectives without becoming fatigued by the enormity of the task at hand.

3. Cultivate a Positive Environment
Surrounding yourself with a supportive environment is essential for sustaining energy. This includes both physical and social aspects. A clutter-free workspace can enhance focus and efficiency, while a supportive social network can inspire and motivate you during challenging times. Engaging with like-minded individuals who share similar financial aspirations can energize your efforts and provide valuable support. Consider joining professional groups, attending seminars, or participating in online forums related to your financial interests.

4. Practice Mindfulness and Stress Management
High levels of stress can drain your energy and hinder productivity. Practices such as mindfulness, meditation, or yoga can help manage stress effectively. Mindfulness encourages you to remain present, reducing anxiety about future financial uncertainties.

Developing a regular practice of mindfulness or relaxation techniques not only helps in maintaining emotional balance but also enhances overall mental clarity and focus, which are essential for sustained energy.

5. Engage in Continuous Learning

Staying engaged and curious can significantly boost your energy. When you continually seek knowledge and skills pertinent to your financial goals, you maintain a sense of purpose and enthusiasm. Attend workshops, read books, or listen to podcasts that inspire you and expand your understanding of wealth-building strategies. This ongoing education can invigorate your passion for your financial journey and keep your energy levels high.

6. Monitor and Adjust Your Goals

As you progress toward your financial objectives, regularly review and adjust your goals to reflect changing circumstances or new insights. This adaptability can prevent burnout and maintain motivation, ensuring that you remain aligned with your values and aspirations. If certain goals become too daunting or irrelevant, adjust them to be more achievable, allowing for sustained energy and focus on what truly matters to you.

7. Prioritize Self-Care

Finally, self-care is crucial in maintaining energy levels. Engage in activities that rejuvenate you, whether it's pursuing a hobby, spending time with loved ones, or simply enjoying quiet time. Recognizing the importance of personal well-being ensures that you have the emotional and physical stamina to pursue your long-term financial objectives without feeling drained.

In conclusion, sustaining energy for long-term success in wealth-building is a multifaceted endeavor. By establishing a balanced routine, cultivating a positive environment, practicing mindfulness, engaging in continuous learning, and prioritizing self-care, you create a solid foundation that allows you to pursue your financial goals with vigor and resilience.

Chapter 12

ENGAGING THE SUBCONSCIOUS FOR ACHIEVEMENT

The Subconscious Mind's Role in Wealth

The subconscious mind plays a pivotal role in shaping our financial reality, influencing our behaviors, decisions, and ultimately our wealth. It operates below the level of conscious awareness, storing our beliefs, experiences, and emotions. Understanding the subconscious mind's influence on wealth is crucial for anyone seeking financial success, as it can either propel them toward their goals or serve as a barrier to achieving them.

The Nature of the Subconscious Mind

The subconscious mind is responsible for managing our automatic functions and responses. It absorbs and processes information continuously, often without our conscious knowledge. This includes our internalized beliefs about money, success, and self-worth. For instance, if someone was raised in an environment where money was viewed negatively or associated with greed, their subconscious may carry these beliefs into adulthood, leading to financial self-sabotage. Such ingrained beliefs can manifest as fear of success, reluctance to pursue lucrative opportunities, or even behaviors that undermine financial stability.

The Impact of Subconscious Beliefs on Financial Outcomes

Subconscious beliefs create a framework through which we interpret our financial reality. These beliefs dictate our comfort level with money, shaping our responses to wealth-related situations. For example, a person who believes they are unworthy of financial abundance may unconsciously avoid opportunities that could lead to increased income, or they may find themselves in situations that reinforce their negative beliefs about money.

Moreover, the subconscious mind heavily influences our decision-making processes. When faced with financial choices, it is often the subconscious that guides us, based on past experiences and beliefs. If one has a deep-seated belief that making money is difficult or that wealth comes at the expense of personal integrity, they may find themselves paralyzed when it comes to taking action toward financial goals. On the other hand, a strong belief in one's ability to create wealth can lead to proactive decision-making and the pursuit of growth opportunities.

Programming the Subconscious for Success
To leverage the power of the subconscious mind for financial success, it is essential to engage in practices that promote positive belief systems. One effective method is through the use of affirmations and visualization techniques. By consistently repeating affirmations that reinforce a positive mindset about wealth, individuals can begin to reshape their subconscious beliefs. For example, affirmations like "I am worthy of financial abundance" or "I attract opportunities for wealth" can help replace limiting beliefs with empowering ones.

Visualization is another powerful tool. By vividly imagining oneself achieving financial goals—whether it be owning a successful business, enjoying financial freedom, or living a life of abundance—individuals can create a mental image that their subconscious can work towards manifesting in reality. This process helps to align subconscious programming with conscious financial aspirations.

Identifying and Changing Subconscious Patterns
Recognizing and altering negative subconscious patterns is vital for fostering a mindset conducive to wealth. This can be achieved through introspection and mindfulness practices. Journaling about financial experiences and emotions can reveal negative beliefs that may be influencing behaviors. Once identified, these beliefs can be challenged and reframed. For instance, if someone identifies a belief that "money is hard to come by," they can reframe it to "money flows easily to me when I create value."

Additionally, working with a coach or therapist who specializes in financial psychology can provide valuable insights and strategies for overcoming subconscious barriers to wealth.

Conclusion
In conclusion, the subconscious mind is a powerful force in shaping our financial outcomes. By understanding its role and actively working to program it with positive beliefs about wealth, individuals can break free from limiting patterns and move toward financial prosperity. Embracing this journey involves continuous self-awareness and a commitment to reshaping the beliefs that govern our financial decisions. As we align our subconscious with our conscious financial goals, we pave the way for greater wealth and abundance in our lives.

Programming the Subconscious for Success
The subconscious mind plays a pivotal role in shaping our reality, influencing our thoughts, behaviors, and, ultimately, our financial outcomes. To achieve wealth, it is crucial to program the

subconscious to align with your financial aspirations. This programming process involves various techniques that can help rewire your mental pathways, fostering an environment conducive to success.

1. Understanding the Subconscious Mind

The subconscious mind operates beneath our conscious awareness, processing information, emotions, and experiences that can strongly influence our decisions and actions. It holds beliefs, fears, and habits that we may not even realize are affecting our financial pursuits. By consciously programming this aspect of our mind, we can replace limiting beliefs with empowering ones, paving the way for wealth-building opportunities.

2. Visualization Techniques

One of the most effective techniques for programming the subconscious mind is visualization. This involves creating detailed mental images of your financial goals and the lifestyle you desire. Spend time each day visualizing yourself achieving your financial objectives, whether it's landing a lucrative job, launching a successful business, or enjoying the financial freedom to travel the world. The key is to engage all your senses in this process:

- **Sight**: Picture the environment and experiences that accompany your success.
- **Sound**: Imagine the sounds that would be present, such as applause for your achievements or the chatter of friends celebrating with you.
- **Touch**: Feel the textures associated with your success, such as the firmness of a handshake after closing a deal or the smoothness of a new car's steering wheel.

By immersing yourself in these vivid mental experiences, you signal to your subconscious mind that these goals are not only possible but also your reality.

3. Affirmations for Financial Success

Another powerful tool for subconscious programming is the use of affirmations. These are positive statements that reflect your financial goals and aspirations. To be effective, affirmations should be:

- **Present Tense**: Phrase affirmations as if they are already happening. For example, "I am attracting wealth effortlessly" instead of "I will attract wealth."
- **Specific**: The more specific your affirmation, the more effective it becomes. Instead of saying "I am wealthy," you could say, "I have a net worth of one million dollars by the age of 30."
- **Emotionally Charged**: Choose words that evoke strong, positive emotions, reinforcing your commitment to these beliefs.

Repeat these affirmations daily, ideally in a relaxed state, such as during meditation or just before sleep, when the subconscious is most receptive.

4. Meditation and Mindfulness

Incorporating meditation and mindfulness practices into your routine can significantly enhance your ability to program the subconscious mind. These practices create a mental space where you can observe your thoughts without judgment, allowing you to identify limiting beliefs and replace them with constructive ones. Guided meditations focused on financial abundance can be particularly beneficial, helping you cultivate a mindset aligned with wealth.

5. Creating a Vision Board

A vision board is a tangible representation of your financial goals. It consists of images, quotes, and reminders that embody your aspirations. By regularly viewing your vision board, you create a constant reminder of what you're working towards, embedding these images deeper into your subconscious. This visual stimulus can trigger feelings of motivation and excitement, reinforcing your commitment to your financial journey.

6. Consistent Review and Adjustment

Programming the subconscious is not a one-time event; it requires consistent effort. Regularly review your goals, affirmations, and visualization practices to ensure they remain aligned with your evolving aspirations. Adjust your techniques as needed, ensuring that your subconscious programming stays relevant and effective.

By employing these techniques, you can effectively program your subconscious mind to support your journey toward financial success, transforming your beliefs and behaviors in alignment with your wealth-building goals. The combination of visualization, affirmations, meditation, and consistent review creates a powerful framework for achieving the financial life you desire.

Identifying and Changing Subconscious Patterns

The subconscious mind plays a pivotal role in shaping our behaviors, thoughts, and ultimately, our financial outcomes. It is a reservoir of beliefs and experiences, often formed during childhood, that influence our decisions and reactions in adulthood. Understanding and altering negative subconscious patterns can be a transformative process, allowing individuals to unlock their full potential for wealth and success.

Identifying Negative Subconscious Patterns

The first step in changing negative subconscious patterns is to identify them. This requires introspection and self-awareness. Common indicators of negative subconscious beliefs include recurring self-sabotaging behaviors, persistent feelings of inadequacy, and a tendency to avoid financial opportunities. Here are some strategies to recognize these patterns:

1. Journaling: Keeping a journal can help track thoughts and feelings related to money. By writing down daily financial decisions and the emotions tied to them, individuals can identify recurring themes and underlying beliefs that may hinder their financial success.

2. Reflection on Past Experiences: Analyzing past financial decisions and their outcomes can provide clues about subconscious beliefs. For instance, if someone consistently avoids investing due to a fear of loss, it may stem from a belief formed in childhood about money being scarce or dangerous.

3. Emotional Triggers: Pay attention to emotional reactions when faced with financial decisions. Feelings of anxiety, guilt, or shame can indicate deep-seated beliefs that need addressing.

4. Feedback from Others: Sometimes, friends or family can offer insights into our behavior that we might overlook. Constructive feedback can help shine a light on subconscious patterns that affect financial choices.

Changing Negative Subconscious Patterns

Once negative patterns are identified, the next step is to change them. This process involves reprogramming the subconscious mind through various techniques:

1. Affirmations: Positive affirmations can counteract negative beliefs. For instance, replacing "I will never be rich" with "I am capable of achieving financial success" can gradually reshape one's subconscious beliefs. It's vital to repeat these affirmations regularly, ideally in a calm and focused state, to reinforce new thought patterns.

2. Visualization: Visualization techniques enable individuals to imagine themselves achieving their financial goals. By creating vivid mental images of success and abundance, one can train the subconscious to accept these scenarios as possible realities. This practice can involve visualizing oneself enjoying the fruits of financial success, such as living in a dream home or traveling to desired destinations.

3. Meditation and Mindfulness: Engaging in meditation can help quiet the mind and create a space for self-reflection. Mindfulness practices can aid in recognizing negative thoughts as they arise, allowing individuals to consciously redirect their focus towards more positive, empowering thoughts about wealth and success.

4. Hypnotherapy: For those deeply entrenched in negative subconscious patterns, hypnotherapy can be an effective solution. A trained hypnotherapist can guide individuals into a relaxed state where they can explore and alter deep-seated beliefs, providing a pathway to reprogram the subconscious mind.

5. Surrounding Yourself with Positivity: The company we keep significantly influences our subconscious beliefs. Engaging with positive, like-minded individuals can foster an environment conducive to growth and success. This support network can reinforce new beliefs and encourage accountability.

Conclusion

Identifying and changing negative subconscious patterns is essential for anyone seeking financial success. By employing strategies such as journaling, affirmations, and visualization, individuals can uncover and alter the beliefs that hinder their progress. This transformative process not only enhances one's financial mindset but also paves the way for a more fulfilling and prosperous life. Ultimately, the journey to wealth begins with understanding and reshaping the subconscious beliefs that dictate our actions.

Chapter 13

ENHANCING MENTAL CAPABILITIES

Improving Cognitive Functions for Better Decisions

In the pursuit of wealth, the ability to make sound financial decisions is paramount. Cognitive functions—such as memory, attention, reasoning, and problem-solving—play a critical role in decision-making processes. To enhance these capabilities, individuals can adopt a variety of strategies that promote better mental acuity, ultimately leading to more informed and effective financial choices.

1. Prioritize Mental Health
Mental acuity is closely linked to overall mental health. Stress, anxiety, and fatigue can significantly impair cognitive functions. Therefore, prioritizing mental well-being is essential. Techniques such as mindfulness meditation, yoga, and regular physical exercise can help alleviate stress and improve focus. Engaging in these activities not only enhances emotional resilience but also sharpens cognitive abilities, allowing for clearer thinking during financial decision-making.

2. Engage in Continuous Learning
A commitment to lifelong learning can significantly enhance cognitive functions. By regularly exposing the brain to new information, individuals can strengthen neural pathways, thereby improving memory and critical thinking skills. Reading books, attending workshops, and taking online courses related to finance, economics, or personal development can foster a deeper understanding of complex financial concepts. Furthermore,

discussions with knowledgeable peers can provide fresh perspectives and stimulate cognitive engagement.

3. Practice Problem-Solving Skills

Problem-solving is a key component of effective decision-making. Engaging in activities that challenge the mind, such as puzzles, strategy games, or even coding, can enhance analytical thinking and improve the ability to assess various financial scenarios. Regularly practicing these skills can build a habit of approaching financial challenges with a systematic and logical mindset.

4. Maintain a Balanced Diet

Nutrition plays a vital role in cognitive functioning. A well-balanced diet rich in omega-3 fatty acids, antioxidants, vitamins, and minerals supports brain health. Foods such as fatty fish, nuts, berries, leafy greens, and whole grains can enhance memory and cognitive performance. Staying hydrated is equally important, as dehydration can lead to confusion and impaired cognitive abilities. Thus, maintaining proper nutrition is an essential strategy for improving mental acuity.

5. Get Adequate Sleep

Sleep is crucial for cognitive functions. During sleep, the brain consolidates and organizes information, which is essential for memory retention and decision-making. Aim for 7-9 hours of quality sleep each night to ensure optimal cognitive performance. Establishing a regular sleep routine, reducing screen time before bed, and creating a calming bedtime environment can facilitate better sleep quality.

6. Foster Social Connections

Social interactions stimulate cognitive functions, as engaging conversations and debates challenge the mind and encourage critical thinking. Building a network of like-minded individuals who share similar financial goals can provide support and diverse viewpoints that can enhance decision-making. Participating in group discussions or attending networking events can foster relationships that encourage cognitive growth.

7. Utilize Technology Wisely

In the age of information, leveraging technology can improve cognitive functions. Various apps and tools can help track expenses, set financial goals, and analyze investment opportunities. Utilizing financial software can streamline decision-making processes by providing clear insights and data-driven guidance. However, it's essential to remain mindful of information overload, as excessive information can lead to decision paralysis.

Conclusion

Improving cognitive functions is a multifaceted approach that involves prioritizing mental health, engaging in continuous learning, practicing problem-solving, maintaining a balanced diet, ensuring adequate sleep, fostering social connections, and wisely utilizing technology. By implementing these strategies, individuals can enhance their mental acuity, leading to more effective financial decisions and ultimately paving the way for greater wealth accumulation.

Techniques to Boost Focus and Clarity

Achieving financial success necessitates a clear and focused mind. Concentration and mental clarity are essential tools for making informed decisions, devising strategies, and executing plans effectively. Below are some techniques designed to enhance focus and clarity, enabling individuals to navigate their financial journeys with confidence.

1. Establish a Dedicated Workspace:
Creating a designated area for financial planning and decision-making can significantly enhance focus. This space should be free from distractions and clutter, fostering an environment conducive to concentration. Consider incorporating elements that inspire productivity, such as motivational quotes, vision boards, or calming colors. A consistent workspace signals to your mind that it's time to engage in focused financial activities.

2. Set Clear Goals and Priorities:
Before embarking on any financial tasks, spend time defining clear, specific goals. Write down your objectives and prioritize them based on urgency and importance. This practice not only provides a structured roadmap but also eliminates ambiguity, allowing for better focus on each individual task. By knowing what to tackle first, you can direct your mental energy effectively.

3. Utilize Time Management Techniques:
Employing time management strategies, such as the Pomodoro Technique, can enhance focus. This method involves working for 25 minutes and then taking a 5-minute break. The structured intervals help maintain high levels of concentration while preventing mental fatigue. During breaks, engage in activities that recharge your energy, such as stretching or deep breathing exercises.

4. Practice Mindfulness and Meditation:
Mindfulness practices can improve concentration and mental clarity by training your brain to stay present in the moment.

Regular meditation can enhance cognitive functions and reduce distractions. Aim for at least 10 minutes of meditation daily, focusing on your breath or a calming mantra. Over time, this practice can help cultivate a more focused mindset and improve your ability to think clearly under pressure.

5. Limit Digital Distractions:
In an age dominated by technology, digital distractions can severely impact focus. Set boundaries around technology usage, especially during financial planning sessions. Use apps that block distracting websites or notifications during dedicated work periods. Consider scheduling specific times to check emails or social media, allowing for uninterrupted focus during critical financial tasks.

6. Maintain a Healthy Lifestyle:
Physical well-being directly influences mental clarity. Regular exercise boosts blood flow to the brain, enhancing cognitive functions. A balanced diet rich in omega-3 fatty acids, antioxidants, and whole grains supports brain health. Additionally, ensuring adequate sleep is crucial; lack of sleep can lead to decreased focus and impaired decision-making. Strive for 7-9 hours of quality sleep each night to maintain optimal cognitive performance.

7. Engage in Brain-Boosting Activities:
Incorporate activities that stimulate your brain and improve cognitive functions. Puzzles, strategy games, or even learning a new skill can sharpen your mental acuity. Regularly engaging in these activities strengthens neural connections, enhancing your ability to concentrate and think clearly.

8. Adopt a Growth Mindset:
Embrace a growth mindset, which encourages viewing challenges as opportunities for learning rather than obstacles. This perspective can alleviate stress and enhance focus on solutions rather than problems. Cultivating resilience through a growth mindset can also help maintain clarity when faced with financial setbacks.

In conclusion, boosting focus and clarity is not merely about improving concentration; it's about creating an environment and mindset conducive to effective financial decision-making. By implementing these techniques, individuals can enhance their cognitive abilities, streamline their financial planning processes, and ultimately make more informed choices that lead to sustainable wealth accumulation. Regular practice of these strategies can cultivate a sharp, focused mind capable of overcoming the complexities of financial challenges.

Applying Mental Sharpness to Spot Opportunities

In the journey towards wealth accumulation, one of the most critical skills an individual can develop is the ability to recognize and seize financial opportunities. This skill is often contingent upon mental sharpness, which encompasses cognitive clarity, analytical prowess, and a keen awareness of the environment. By honing these mental faculties, individuals can enhance their capacity to identify lucrative opportunities that may otherwise go unnoticed.

Cultivating Mental Clarity

Mental clarity is the foundation of sharp cognitive functioning. It allows individuals to filter out distractions and focus on the essentials. To cultivate mental clarity, individuals can employ various techniques:

1. **Mindfulness Meditation**: Practicing mindfulness can enhance awareness and concentration. By training the mind to be present, individuals can improve their ability to observe details and recognize patterns that indicate potential financial opportunities.

2. **Journaling**: Keeping a daily journal can help clarify thoughts and feelings. By writing down ideas, reflections, and observations about financial markets or personal ventures, individuals can organize their thoughts and identify recurring themes or opportunities that may require action.

3. **Limit Information Overload**: In today's digital age, information is abundant, and this can lead to cognitive overload. Prioritizing sources of information and setting aside time to absorb that information can lead to deeper understanding and better opportunity recognition.

Enhancing Analytical Thinking

Analytical thinking involves the ability to dissect information and evaluate it critically. To boost analytical skills, consider the following strategies:

1. **Practice Critical Thinking**: Engage in exercises that challenge your reasoning, such as puzzles, strategy games, or even debates on financial topics. This practice can sharpen your analytical skills and improve your ability to assess potential opportunities quickly.

2. **Scenario Analysis**: When evaluating potential investments or business ideas, conduct a thorough scenario analysis. Consider best-case, worst-case, and most likely outcomes. This practice not only sharpens analytical skills; it also prepares individuals to act decisively when opportunities arise.

3. Financial Literacy: Understanding financial principles, such as cash flow management, investment strategies, and market dynamics, enhances one's ability to analyze opportunities effectively. Continuous learning through books, courses, or seminars can bolster financial acumen.

Developing a Keen Awareness

A keen awareness of one's surroundings and market dynamics is essential for spotting opportunities. This can be developed through:

1. Networking: Engaging with professionals in various industries can provide insights into emerging trends and opportunities. Attending industry conferences, seminars, or informal networking events can foster connections that may lead to lucrative opportunities.

2. Real-Time Market Analysis: Keeping abreast of financial news, market trends, and economic indicators can help individuals identify shifts in the market that may present new opportunities. Tools such as financial news apps, stock market trackers, and economic forecasts can be invaluable.

3. Feedback and Reflection: After making decisions, reflect on the outcomes and seek feedback. This process can help identify what worked well and what didn't, sharpening awareness and improving future decision-making.

Seizing Opportunities with Confidence

Once an opportunity has been identified, the ability to act decisively is paramount. Mental sharpness not only aids in recognizing opportunities but also in having the confidence to pursue them. This can be achieved by:

1. Setting Clear Goals: Having specific, measurable goals can provide clarity and focus, making it easier to recognize when an opportunity aligns with those objectives.

2. Creating a Decision-Making Framework: Establish a personal framework for decision-making that includes criteria for evaluating opportunities. This will streamline the process and reduce hesitation when it comes time to act.

In conclusion, applying mental sharpness to spot financial opportunities involves cultivating mental clarity, enhancing analytical thinking, and developing keen awareness. By investing in these cognitive skills, individuals can significantly improve their ability to recognize and seize opportunities, ultimately paving the way for greater financial success.

Chapter 14

RELYING ON INTUITION IN FINANCIAL MATTERS

Understanding Intuition's Role in Wealth Building

Intuition, often described as a gut feeling or an instinctive understanding, plays a pivotal role in financial decision-making and wealth building. While traditional financial analysis involves a methodical approach, relying on data and structured reasoning, intuition serves as a complementary tool that can enhance our decision-making capabilities. The essence of intuition lies in its ability to synthesize vast amounts of information, experiences, and emotional cues into actionable insights, often without the individual being fully aware of the underlying processes.

The Nature of Intuition

Intuition is rooted in our subconscious mind, where myriad experiences and knowledge reside. This reservoir of information allows us to make quick judgments and decisions based on patterns we may not consciously recognize. For instance, an investor may feel a strong inclination to buy a particular stock based on a hunch, which could stem from previous experiences, market trends, or even emotional responses to news. While this decision may lack rigorous analytical backing, it can be informed by a wealth of personal and historical context.

The Science Behind Intuition

Research in psychology and neuroscience suggests that intuition arises from the brain's ability to recognize patterns and make predictions. Studies have shown that individuals often rely on their intuitive judgments, especially in high-stakes situations, where time is limited and the cost of indecision is significant. This rapid processing can be particularly beneficial in financial settings, where market conditions shift quickly and opportunities can be fleeting.

Furthermore, the brain's emotional centers, such as the amygdala, play a role in intuitive decision-making. Emotions are integral to how we perceive and respond to financial situations. A positive gut feeling about an investment can lead to a decision that aligns with one's financial goals, while a negative feeling may serve as a warning sign to reevaluate a potential risk.

Developing and Trusting Your Intuitive Sense
To harness the power of intuition in wealth building, it is essential to cultivate and trust this inner guidance. Here are several strategies to help develop a stronger intuitive sense:

1. Self-Reflection: Regularly engage in self-reflection to understand your emotional responses and past financial decisions. Journaling can be a helpful tool for this practice, allowing you to track your feelings and the outcomes of decisions made based on intuition.

2. Mindfulness and Meditation: Techniques such as mindfulness and meditation can enhance your ability to connect with your intuitive self. These practices promote a calm mental state, enabling you to tune into your gut feelings without the interference of stress or anxiety.

3. Experience and Exposure: The more exposure you have to various financial situations, the sharper your intuition will become.

Attend workshops, read extensively about market dynamics, and engage with diverse financial scenarios, as this will build a robust foundation for intuitive insights.

4. Listening to Your Body: Pay attention to physical sensations that accompany your intuitive feelings. Often, our bodies react to situations before our conscious mind processes them. Notice any tension, excitement, or discomfort that arises when considering financial decisions.

Balancing Logic and Instinct

While intuition can guide financial decisions, it is crucial to balance it with rational analysis. A well-rounded approach to wealth building incorporates both intuitive insights and analytical thinking. By validating gut feelings with research and data, individuals can make informed decisions while still remaining open to instinctual guidance.

In conclusion, intuition is a powerful ally in the journey toward financial success. By understanding and developing this innate ability, individuals can enhance their decision-making processes, capitalize on opportunities, and navigate the complexities of wealth building with greater confidence. Embracing intuition does not diminish the importance of analytical skills; rather, it enriches the overall approach to financial growth, leading to more nuanced and effective decision-making.

Developing and Trusting Your Intuitive Sense

Intuition, often described as a gut feeling or instinct, is a powerful tool in financial decision-making. It acts as an internal compass, guiding us toward opportunities or warning us against potential pitfalls. While data and analytics are essential for informed choices, harnessing intuition can enhance decision-making by incorporating a holistic understanding of situations. This section explores practical methods to enhance and rely on your intuitive sense in financial matters.

1. Cultivating Awareness of Intuitive Signals
The first step in developing your intuitive sense is to cultivate awareness. Intuition often manifests through physical sensations, emotional responses, or sudden insights. To recognize these signals, practice mindfulness and self-reflection. Regular meditation or deep-breathing exercises can heighten your awareness of your internal states. By creating moments of stillness, you can better distinguish between intuitive signals and emotional noise, allowing you to respond to genuine gut feelings.

Exercise: Spend a few minutes each day in quiet reflection. Ask yourself about a financial decision you need to make, and observe any physical sensations or emotions that arise. Record these impressions in a journal to identify patterns over time.

2. Engaging in Reflective Practices
Engaging in reflective practices helps connect past experiences with your intuitive insights. After making financial decisions, take time to reflect on the process: What were your gut feelings? Did they align with the outcome? By assessing the correlation between your intuition and results, you can build confidence in trusting your instincts.

Exercise: After each financial decision, regardless of the outcome, write down your initial intuitive feelings before making the choice and how you felt afterward. This reflection reinforces the relationship between intuition and decision-making.

3. Creating a Decision Framework

Developing a structured decision-making framework can aid in balancing intuition with rational analysis. This framework should integrate both intuitive insights and logical reasoning, allowing for a comprehensive evaluation of choices. For instance, when considering an investment, assess the quantitative aspects (like ROI and market trends) alongside qualitative factors (like your gut feeling about the business or its leadership).

Exercise: Create a decision matrix that lists both logical criteria and intuitive feelings. Rate each criterion to see how they align. This method ensures that you give weight to your instincts while still adhering to analytical standards.

4. Trusting Your Instincts Through Small Decisions

To build confidence in your intuition, start by applying it to smaller, less consequential decisions. This could involve choosing investments in a low-risk environment or selecting new suppliers based on gut feelings. By validating your intuition through smaller choices, you can gradually develop trust in your instincts.

Exercise: Make a series of small financial decisions based solely on your instinct. Monitor the outcomes and reflect upon these experiences. Over time, this practice will strengthen your confidence in relying on intuition for larger choices.

5. Balancing Intuition with Research

While intuition is valuable, it should not replace thorough research and analysis. Instead, use intuition as a complementary tool. After conducting research, take a moment to pause and listen to your gut feeling about the situation. Does it align with the data? If not, consider exploring the dissonance further.

Exercise: After completing a research phase for a financial decision, set aside time to engage in a "gut check." Close your eyes, visualize the decision at hand, and note any intuitive feelings. This practice promotes an integrative approach to decision-making.

6. Learning from Experience
Finally, recognize that developing intuitive sense is a journey that evolves through experience. Each financial decision, whether successful or not, provides valuable lessons. Embrace the learning process and remain open to refining your intuitive abilities as you grow and adapt in your financial journey.

By enhancing and trusting your intuitive sense, you can navigate the complexities of financial decision-making with greater confidence and clarity. Balancing intuitive insights with logical analysis creates a powerful synergy that can lead to more effective wealth-building strategies.

Balancing Logic and Instinct in Choices

In the pursuit of financial success, individuals often grapple with the dichotomy between analytical reasoning and intuitive insights. While traditional financial education emphasizes the importance of data-driven decision-making, it is equally critical to acknowledge the role of intuition. Striking a balance between logical analysis and instinctual understanding can lead to more holistic and effective decision-making processes. This section will explore strategies to integrate these two dimensions, allowing individuals to make sound financial choices.

1. Acknowledge the Value of Both Approaches

The first step in balancing logic and instinct is to recognize that both are valuable in their own right. Analytical thinking is grounded in facts, historical data, and structured methodologies, making it indispensable for assessing risks and forecasting outcomes. Conversely, intuition draws from subconscious experiences and emotional responses, often providing insights that may not be immediately evident through rational analysis. By acknowledging the strengths of both approaches, individuals can create a more rounded perspective when faced with financial decisions.

2. Develop a Framework for Decision-Making

Creating a structured framework can help individuals systematically evaluate their options while leaving room for intuitive insights. This might involve a decision-making matrix that includes quantitative factors—such as cost, potential return on investment, and market trends—alongside qualitative aspects like gut feelings, personal values, and emotional responses to potential outcomes. By laying out the pros and cons in a visual format, decision-makers can analyze the situation logically while also considering their instincts.

3. Practice Mindfulness and Reflection

Mindfulness practices can enhance one's ability to listen to their intuition. By cultivating a state of awareness, individuals can better tune into their subconscious feelings about a decision. Techniques such as meditation, journaling, or simply spending time in nature can provide clarity and help separate intuitive insights from emotional biases. Reflecting on previous decisions, both successful and unsuccessful, can also illuminate patterns in how intuition has played a role in past outcomes, aiding future decision-making.

4. Conduct Scenario Analysis

Scenario analysis involves envisioning multiple potential outcomes based on different decisions. By contemplating various scenarios, individuals can engage their analytical side to evaluate the logical implications of each path. At the same time, they can pay attention to how these scenarios resonate on an intuitive level. For instance, if a particular scenario feels uncomfortable despite appearing beneficial on paper, it may warrant further investigation or a reconsideration of the decision.

5. Seek External Perspectives

Sometimes, our own biases can cloud judgment, making it challenging to balance logic and instinct. Seeking the perspectives of trusted advisors or peers can provide valuable insights that may align with intuitive feelings. Engaging in discussions with individuals who have faced similar financial decisions can surface instinctual wisdom that complements analytical assessments. Moreover, collaborative decision-making fosters an environment where diverse viewpoints can challenge and refine one's thought processes.

6. Implement a Decision Review Process

After making a financial decision, it is crucial to evaluate the outcomes and reflect on the decision-making process. Did the logical analysis hold up? Were there intuitive hints that should have been heeded? This reflective practice allows individuals to learn from their experiences, reinforcing the importance of balancing logic and instinct in future choices. Over time, this iterative process can enhance one's ability to make sound decisions, blending analytical rigor with instinctual guidance.

Conclusion

Balancing logic and instinct in financial decision-making is not merely about choosing one approach over the other; it is about recognizing the interplay between them. By embracing both analytical reasoning and intuitive insights, individuals can enhance their capacity for sound financial choices. Implementing structured frameworks, practicing mindfulness, seeking external insights, and reflecting on decisions can create a comprehensive approach to decision-making that paves the way for greater financial success and personal fulfillment.

Recognizing and Overcoming Intuitive Blocks

Intuition is often described as a gut feeling or an instinctual understanding that guides decision-making without the need for conscious reasoning. While intuition can be a powerful asset in financial matters, many individuals find their ability to tap into their intuitive insights hindered by various blocks. Recognizing and overcoming these intuitive blocks is essential for harnessing the full potential of intuitive thinking in wealth-building endeavors.

Identifying Intuitive Blocks

1. Fear and Anxiety: One of the most significant barriers to intuitive thinking is fear. Fear of failure, fear of making the wrong decision, or fear of judgment can cloud our judgment and lead to overthinking. This anxiety can create a mental fog that obscures intuitive insights, making it challenging to discern what feels right. Recognizing the specific fears that trigger these reactions is the first step toward overcoming them.

2. Self-Doubt: Many individuals struggle with self-doubt, questioning their judgment and abilities. This lack of confidence can stifle intuition, leading to second-guessing and indecision. When we doubt our instincts, we often rely too heavily on external validation or data, which can divert attention from our inner guidance.

3. Over-Reliance on Logic: In a world that often prioritizes data-driven decision-making, it can be easy to dismiss intuitive feelings as irrational. When logical reasoning becomes the sole criterion for making choices, intuitive nudges may be ignored or undervalued. Striking a balance between analytical thinking and intuitive insights is crucial for effective decision-making.

4. External Influences: The opinions and expectations of others can create noise that interferes with our intuition. When surrounded by conflicting viewpoints or societal norms, individuals may struggle to hear their inner voice. This external pressure can lead to conformity rather than authentic decision-making based on personal intuition.

5. Disconnection from Self: A lack of self-awareness often results from a fast-paced lifestyle that prioritizes external tasks over internal reflection. When individuals do not take the time to connect with their thoughts and feelings, they may miss important intuitive signals. This disconnection can stem from stress, busyness, or a lack of mindfulness practices.

Addressing Intuitive Blocks

1. Cultivating Mindfulness: Practicing mindfulness is one of the most effective ways to enhance intuition. Mindfulness encourages individuals to become more aware of their thoughts, feelings, and bodily sensations, creating space for intuitive insights to emerge.

Techniques such as meditation, deep breathing, and journaling can help cultivate a sense of presence, allowing individuals to tune into their inner guidance.

2. **Challenging Fears**: Addressing fears directly can help dismantle their hold. Individuals can benefit from identifying specific fears that block their intuition and challenging their validity. Techniques such as cognitive-behavioral therapy (CBT) can help reframe negative thought patterns, fostering a more resilient mindset. Exposure to the source of fear, in a controlled and supportive environment, can also help reduce its power.

3. **Building Self-Confidence**: Enhancing self-confidence is vital for overcoming self-doubt. Individuals can start by acknowledging past successes and recognizing their strengths. Engaging in activities that promote skill development and competence can bolster confidence, making it easier to trust intuitive insights.

4. **Creating Space for Reflection**: Setting aside time for reflection and self-discovery can deepen the connection to one's intuition. This can involve quiet moments of solitude, engaging in creative activities, or seeking nature's tranquility. Journaling thoughts and feelings can also facilitate clarity, allowing intuitive thoughts to surface.

5. **Limiting External Noise**: Reducing exposure to outside opinions or pressures can help clear the mental clutter that obstructs intuition. This may involve setting boundaries with overly critical individuals or limiting consumption of media that fosters doubt. Instead, surrounding oneself with supportive, like-minded individuals can create an environment conducive to intuitive thinking.

Recognizing and overcoming intuitive blocks is a dynamic process that requires self-awareness, practice, and patience. By identifying the specific barriers that hinder intuitive thinking and employing strategies to address them, individuals can unlock their innate ability to make sound financial decisions guided by their intuition. This journey towards embracing intuition can lead to not only better financial outcomes but also a more enriched and fulfilling life.

Applying Intuition to Seize Opportunities

Intuition, often described as a gut feeling or instinct, plays a pivotal role in navigating the complex landscape of financial opportunities. In the realm of wealth building, honing this instinct can be a game changer, allowing individuals to identify lucrative prospects that may not be immediately apparent through analytical reasoning alone. This section delves into the significance of intuition in decision-making, strategies for enhancing intuitive capabilities, and practical steps for translating intuitive insights into actionable financial outcomes.

The Essence of Intuition in Financial Decision-Making

Intuition is a product of accumulated experiences, knowledge, and subconscious processing. It synthesizes information from past encounters, enabling individuals to make quick decisions based on patterns and cues that may not be consciously recognized. In financial matters, this can manifest as an innate sense of timing—knowing when to invest, when to hold back, or when to pivot strategies. By trusting and refining this instinct, individuals can gain a competitive edge, especially in fast-paced markets where data alone may not provide sufficient clarity.

Developing and Trusting Your Intuitive Sense

To leverage intuition effectively, one must first cultivate an awareness of its presence. This begins with mindfulness practices that enhance self-awareness and mental clarity. Techniques such as meditation, journaling, and reflective thinking can create a mental space to listen to one's inner voice. By regularly engaging in these practices, individuals can fine-tune their ability to discern genuine intuitive insights from mere anxiety or external pressure.

Another method is to keep a record of past decisions alongside the feelings associated with them. By analyzing these instances, individuals can identify when intuition led them to success or failure. Over time, this reflective practice builds trust in one's intuitive abilities, fostering a willingness to act on gut feelings in future financial endeavors.

Balancing Logic and Instinct in Choices

While intuition is invaluable, it should not operate in isolation. The most effective decision-making integrates both analytical thinking and intuitive insights. This balance allows individuals to ground their gut feelings in data and rational analysis. For instance, if an intuitive nudge suggests investing in a particular stock, complementing that instinct with thorough research on market trends, company performance, and economic indicators strengthens the decision's foundation.

Moreover, developing a structured decision-making process can help in weighing intuitive insights against logical analysis. Creating a pros and cons list, invoking the "Five Whys" technique, or engaging in scenario planning can provide clarity, helping to distinguish between valuable intuitive prompts and mere impulses.

Recognizing and Overcoming Intuitive Blocks

Despite the potential of intuition, barriers can hinder its effectiveness. Fear, self-doubt, and over-analysis often cloud intuitive judgment. Recognizing these blocks is the first step toward overcoming them. Engaging in cognitive behavioral techniques can help reframe negative thought patterns that disrupt intuitive thinking. For example, if fear of failure inhibits action, visualizing successful outcomes and adopting a growth mindset can mitigate anxiety.

Additionally, surrounding oneself with a supportive network can bolster confidence in intuitive decisions. Sharing ideas with trusted peers can provide validation and encouragement, making it easier to act on intuitive insights.

Applying Intuition to Seize Financial Opportunities

Once individuals have developed their intuitive capabilities and overcome psychological barriers, the next step is to apply these insights actively. When an opportunity arises, whether it be a new investment, a business venture, or a networking chance, pausing to assess intuitive feelings can provide critical guidance. Practicing decisiveness—acting swiftly on these insights—can capitalize on fleeting opportunities that may otherwise be lost.

In conclusion, intuition is a powerful ally in the quest for financial success. By nurturing and trusting this innate faculty, individuals can enhance their ability to identify and seize opportunities, fostering a proactive approach to wealth building. As intuition becomes a trusted partner in decision-making, the path to prosperity becomes clearer, leading to a more fulfilling financial journey.

Chapter 15

OVERCOMING THE SIX MAJOR FEARS

Identifying the Six Common Fears

Fear is an inherent part of the human experience, serving as a primal mechanism for survival. However, in the context of wealth and financial success, fear can become a debilitating barrier. Understanding the prevalent fears that often hinder individuals from pursuing their financial goals is vital. In this section, we will explore six common fears: poverty, criticism, ill health, loss of love, old age, and death, and how they manifest in our lives, particularly in relation to wealth accumulation.

1. Fear of Poverty:
The fear of poverty can paralyze individuals, causing them to avoid risks and opportunities that could lead to financial growth. This fear is often rooted in past experiences, societal conditioning, or family beliefs about money. People may hold on to jobs they dislike or avoid investments due to a deep-seated anxiety about financial instability. This fear can lead to a scarcity mindset, where individuals focus on limitations rather than possibilities, ultimately restricting their financial potential.

2. Fear of Criticism:
The fear of criticism often manifests as a reluctance to take bold actions or pursue unconventional paths that could lead to wealth. Individuals may avoid sharing their ideas or investing in ventures due to the anxiety of being judged by others. This fear can stifle creativity and innovation, which are crucial for financial success. In

a world where entrepreneurial spirit and unique ideas are highly valued, the inability to withstand criticism can prevent individuals from seizing lucrative opportunities.

3. Fear of Ill Health:
Ill health can significantly impact one's ability to generate wealth. The fear of becoming ill can lead individuals to avoid taking risks, whether that means starting a new business, investing in a venture, or pursuing further education. This fear can also result in a preoccupation with security and stability, leading to overly conservative financial choices that may not yield significant returns. Additionally, the financial burden of healthcare can deter individuals from pursuing ambitious financial goals, reinforcing a cycle of fear and inaction.

4. Fear of Loss of Love:
The fear of losing love, whether from family, friends, or significant others, can create anxiety around financial pursuits. People often fear that prioritizing their financial goals may alienate loved ones or lead to relationship conflicts. This fear can result in self-sabotage, where individuals downplay their ambitions to maintain harmony in their personal lives. Consequently, financial aspirations may be compromised, limiting opportunities for growth and success.

5. Fear of Old Age:
As individuals age, the fear of old age can create anxiety about financial security and the ability to sustain oneself in later years. This fear may prompt individuals to hoard wealth, leading to an overly cautious approach to financial management. The dread of becoming a financial burden on others or running out of resources can drive people to make short-term financial decisions that are detrimental to long-term wealth accumulation.

6. Fear of Death:
The fear of death can profoundly affect how individuals perceive their financial goals and legacy. This fear may lead to a focus on immediate gratification rather than long-term planning, as individuals grapple with the impermanence of life. Additionally, concerns about leaving behind debts or financial instability for loved ones can create anxiety that stifles proactive wealth-building efforts.

In conclusion, recognizing these six common fears is the first step toward overcoming them. Acknowledging how these fears influence our financial decisions empowers individuals to confront and address them head-on. By understanding the roots of these fears, one can develop strategies to mitigate their impact and foster a mindset conducive to financial success. Embracing a fearless approach allows individuals to pursue their financial goals with confidence, ultimately leading to greater wealth and fulfillment.

Understanding the Impact of Fear on Success

Fear is a powerful, often paralyzing emotion that can significantly hinder both financial and personal growth. It manifests in various forms and can stem from deep-seated beliefs, societal conditioning, and past experiences. In the pursuit of wealth and prosperity, understanding how fear operates is crucial for overcoming its negative effects and unlocking one's potential.

At the core, fear can be categorized into six major types, each of which can inhibit progress in unique ways. The fear of poverty, for instance, creates a scarcity mindset that can lead individuals to make overly cautious financial decisions. When one is preoccupied with the potential of losing wealth or not having enough, it often results in missed opportunities for investment, entrepreneurship, or even career advancement. This fear can lead to an obsession with saving money rather than utilizing it to generate further wealth.

Similarly, the fear of criticism can stifle creativity and innovation. Individuals may avoid taking calculated risks or pursuing new ideas because they fear being judged or ridiculed by others. This fear can create a conformist mindset, where individuals stick to the status quo instead of exploring new avenues that could lead to financial success. The unwillingness to present one's ideas or take bold actions due to fear of backlash can prevent personal and financial growth.

The fear of ill health can also hinder one's ability to take action towards wealth building. Individuals may become so focused on health concerns that they neglect opportunities for career development or wealth accumulation. This fear can lead to excessive caution in pursuing new ventures, as individuals prioritize safety over potential gain. Consequently, they may miss out on income-generating opportunities simply because they are overly fixated on health-related anxieties.

The fear of loss—whether it be loss of love, social standing, or even personal identity—can also play a critical role in shaping financial behaviors. This fear can drive individuals to make decisions that prioritize short-term comfort and security over long-term financial goals. For example, someone might avoid pursuing a promotion that requires relocation due to fear of losing their current social network, thus sacrificing potential income growth.

As individuals grow older, the fear of old age and death becomes more pronounced. This fear can manifest as a reluctance to take financial risks, leading to overly conservative investment strategies. Many people may cling to security rather than seeking growth opportunities, fearing that they will not have enough resources to sustain themselves in their later years. This protective approach can limit wealth-building potential and lead to stagnation.

Understanding these fears is essential for personal development. The first step in overcoming fear is recognizing its presence and acknowledging its impact on decision-making processes. Once identified, individuals can confront these fears through various strategies. Cognitive-behavioral techniques can help individuals reframe their thoughts, providing a more constructive perspective on risks and opportunities. Developing a proactive mindset that embraces challenges as opportunities for growth can significantly reduce the paralyzing grip of fear.

Moreover, cultivating resilience through mindfulness practices can empower individuals to manage their fears more effectively. Techniques such as meditation, visualization, and positive affirmations can help in building a fearless mindset, allowing individuals to navigate their financial journeys with confidence rather than trepidation.

In conclusion, fear is a formidable barrier to success that can manifest in multiple ways, impacting financial decision-making and personal growth. By understanding its nature and actively working to overcome it, individuals can break free from its constraints, enabling them to pursue wealth and prosperity with a renewed sense of purpose and determination.

Strategies to Conquer Each Fear

Fear is a powerful emotion that can significantly hinder our ability to achieve financial success and overall personal growth. Addressing and conquering the six major fears—poverty, criticism, ill health, loss of love, old age, and death—is essential for anyone aspiring to become rich. This section outlines practical strategies to effectively confront and overcome these fears.

1. Fear of Poverty

The fear of poverty often manifests as a deep-seated anxiety about financial instability. To conquer this fear, begin by reframing your mindset. Shift your focus from scarcity to abundance. Practicing gratitude can help; keep a journal where you regularly note things you're grateful for, particularly in your financial life. Additionally, create a budget that allocates funds for savings and investments, enabling you to feel more secure and in control of your financial future. Educate yourself about money management and investment strategies, which can reduce anxiety and enhance your financial literacy.

2. Fear of Criticism

Fear of criticism can stifle creativity and prevent you from pursuing opportunities. To overcome this fear, adopt a growth mindset that views criticism as constructive feedback rather than personal attacks. Surround yourself with supportive people who encourage your ambitions. When faced with criticism, take a step back and assess its validity. If it's constructive, use it to improve; if it's unfounded, remind yourself of your worth. Practice desensitization by gradually exposing yourself to situations where you might face criticism—whether it's sharing your ideas in a group or seeking feedback on a project.

3. Fear of Ill Health

Concerns about ill health can deter individuals from taking risks or pursuing wealth-building activities. To combat this fear, prioritize your physical and mental well-being. Establish a regular exercise routine, eat a balanced diet, and ensure you get adequate rest. Mindfulness practices like meditation can also enhance your mental resilience. Educate yourself about health issues that concern you, as knowledge can often diminish fear. Create a proactive health plan that includes regular check-ups and preventive measures, empowering you to take control of your health rather than letting fear dictate your actions.

4. Fear of Loss of Love

The fear of losing love, whether from family, friends, or romantic partners, can lead to decision-making paralysis. To overcome this fear, focus on building healthy relationships based on open communication and mutual respect. Reinforce your connections by expressing appreciation and spending quality time with loved ones. Participate in group activities or community service, which can foster a sense of belonging. Remember that real love is resilient; it thrives on authenticity rather than fear-based control.
Acknowledge that pursuing your financial goals may involve making tough choices, but the right relationships will support you through these challenges.

5. Fear of Old Age

The fear of aging often stems from anxiety about losing vitality and financial security. To address this, shift your perspective on aging by embracing it as a stage of growth and wisdom. Create a long-term financial plan that includes retirement savings, thereby alleviating financial anxieties associated with old age. Engage in lifelong learning by taking courses or picking up new hobbies, which can keep your mind active and engaged. Surround yourself with positive role models who demonstrate that aging can be a fulfilling process filled with opportunities.

6. Fear of Death
The fear of death can be overwhelming, particularly regarding legacy and unfulfilled potential. To conquer this fear, focus on living a meaningful life that aligns with your values and aspirations. Engage in conversations about mortality, whether through literature, philosophy, or with trusted friends, to normalize the topic. Establish a personal legacy plan that outlines the impact you wish to leave behind—this could include charitable contributions, mentoring, or sharing your knowledge. By accepting mortality as part of life's journey, you can channel your energy into creating a legacy that outlasts you.

In conclusion, conquering these six major fears requires a proactive approach. By reframing your mindset, prioritizing self-care, and nurturing relationships, you can dismantle the barriers these fears create. Embrace the journey of overcoming them, as it is a vital step toward achieving financial success and personal growth.

Developing a Fearless Mindset

The pursuit of wealth often intersects with one's deepest fears, which can manifest as self-doubt, anxiety, and hesitation. Developing a fearless mindset is essential for overcoming these emotional barriers and forging ahead on the journey to financial success. This section delves into the nuances of cultivating mental resilience, which is crucial for ensuring that fears do not derail your ambitions.

Understanding Fear and Its Impact

Fear is an innate human emotion designed to protect us from harm, but it can also become a hindrance when it leads to procrastination or avoidance of opportunities. Common fears that inhibit wealth-building include the fear of failure, fear of rejection, and even fear of success. Recognizing these fears is the first step toward overcoming them. Acknowledging that these feelings are universal can also help to normalize them, making it easier to confront and manage them.

Cultivating Mental Resilience

1. Mindfulness and Self-Awareness: Practicing mindfulness helps to create space between fear and reaction. By becoming more self-aware, you can identify when fear arises and analyze its root causes without judgment. Mindfulness techniques such as meditation and deep-breathing exercises can help ground you, enabling you to approach challenges with a clearer, more focused mind.

2. Reframing Negative Thoughts: Cognitive reframing involves changing the perspective on fear-inducing situations. Instead of viewing a potential setback as a failure, consider it an opportunity for growth and learning. By framing challenges in a more positive light, you can reduce their emotional weight and build resilience.

3. Setting Incremental Goals: Fear often thrives in ambiguity and overwhelming tasks. By breaking down your financial objectives into smaller, manageable goals, you create a series of achievable milestones. This approach not only makes the journey less daunting but also provides frequent opportunities for success, reinforcing your confidence.

4. Embracing Failure as a Teacher: A crucial aspect of developing a fearless mindset is embracing the inevitability of failure. Rather than viewing mistakes as definitive endpoints, consider them as valuable lessons that contribute to your growth. Analyzing your failures can provide insights that sharpen your future decision-making and inform your approach to wealth-building.

5. Seeking Support: Surrounding yourself with a supportive network can significantly bolster your mental resilience. Connect with mentors, peers, or groups that share similar goals. Engaging in discussions with others who have faced and overcome their fears can provide encouragement and new perspectives, fostering a sense of community in your financial journey.

6. Visualization Techniques: Visualization is a powerful tool in cultivating a fearless mindset. Spend time imagining yourself succeeding, not just in financial terms but also in overcoming fears. Create a mental picture of your goals being achieved, focusing on the positive emotions associated with that success. This practice can help shift your mindset from one of fear to one of anticipation and excitement.

7. Developing a Growth Mindset: Embracing a growth mindset allows you to see challenges as opportunities for development rather than threats. This outlook fosters resilience, as it encourages continuous learning and adaptation. By understanding that abilities and intelligence can be developed through dedication and hard work, you can diminish the power of fear in your financial pursuits.

Conclusion

Cultivating a fearless mindset is an ongoing process that requires dedication and practice. By implementing these strategies, you can build mental resilience that will empower you to navigate the complexities of wealth-building without being hindered by fear. Remember, the journey to prosperity is not just about financial accumulation; it's also about personal growth and embracing the uncertainties that come with it. By developing a fearless approach, you can unlock your full potential and pave the way toward lasting financial success.

Maintaining Progress Despite Challenges

The pursuit of wealth and financial success is often fraught with obstacles, challenges, and fears that can derail even the most determined individuals. To ensure continuous advancement towards financial goals, it is essential to develop strategies for managing and mitigating these fears. This section will explore practical approaches to maintaining progress, even when faced with adversity.

Understanding Challenges and Fears

Challenges are an inherent part of any journey, especially one focused on financial growth. These challenges can manifest in various forms, including unforeseen expenses, economic downturns, or personal setbacks. Accompanying these challenges are fears that often stem from deep-rooted beliefs and past experiences. Common fears such as the fear of failure, fear of criticism, and fear of financial instability can paralyze decision-making and hinder progress.

Recognizing that challenges and fears are normal components of the wealth-building process is the first step in maintaining momentum. Acknowledging their presence allows individuals to prepare mentally and emotionally, instead of being caught off guard when difficulties arise.

Developing a Resilient Mindset

To effectively manage fears and challenges, cultivating a resilient mindset is paramount. Resilience is the ability to bounce back from setbacks, adapt to change, and keep moving forward despite adversity. Here are some strategies to develop this mindset:

1. Reframe Negative Thoughts: Cognitive reframing involves changing the way you interpret challenges. Instead of viewing obstacles as insurmountable, consider them opportunities for growth and learning. This shift in perspective can reduce fear and promote a more positive attitude toward challenges.

2. Embrace a Growth Mindset: Adopting a growth mindset, as coined by psychologist Carol Dweck, entails believing that abilities and intelligence can be developed through dedication and hard work. This mindset encourages individuals to view challenges as pathways to improvement, rather than threats to their success.

3. Set Realistic Expectations: Understand that progress toward financial goals is rarely linear. Setting realistic expectations about the time and effort required can reduce feelings of frustration and disappointment. Break down larger goals into smaller, achievable milestones, celebrating each success along the way.

Building a Support System

A strong support system is crucial for maintaining progress during challenging times. Surrounding oneself with like-minded individuals who share similar financial aspirations can provide motivation and encouragement. Here are ways to build and leverage this network:

- **Seek Mentorship**: Finding a mentor who has successfully navigated their own financial journey can provide invaluable insights and guidance. Mentors can offer advice on overcoming obstacles and instill confidence during difficult periods.

- **Join Communities**: Engaging in communities, whether online or in-person, can foster a sense of belonging and provide emotional support. Sharing experiences with others who understand your challenges can help mitigate fears and reinforce the notion that you are not alone in your journey.

- **Collaborate with Peers**: Partnering with peers on financial projects or goals can create accountability, making it easier to stay on track. Collaboration often leads to shared knowledge, resources, and motivation that can propel all involved toward success.

Practicing Self-Reflection and Adaptation
Continuous self-reflection and adaptation are essential for maintaining progress. Regularly assessing your financial strategies, goals, and emotional responses to challenges can help identify areas for improvement. Consider the following practices:

- **Journaling**: Keeping a financial journal can help track progress, document challenges, and reflect on emotional responses. This practice can clarify feelings, enabling you to confront fears and develop actionable solutions.

- **Mindfulness Techniques**: Engaging in mindfulness practices, such as meditation or deep-breathing exercises, can reduce anxiety and enhance focus. These techniques help create mental space to address fears with clarity and composure.

- **Adjusting Goals**: If certain goals seem increasingly unattainable due to external circumstances, don't hesitate to adjust them. Flexibility in goal-setting ensures that your financial strategies remain realistic and attainable, preventing feelings of defeat.

In conclusion, maintaining progress despite challenges requires a multifaceted approach that combines resilience, support, and adaptability. By actively managing fears and embracing challenges as part of the journey, individuals can ensure continuous advancement toward their financial goals.

www.ingramcontent.com/pod-product-compliance
Lightning Source LLC
LaVergne TN
LVHW012110070526
838202LV00056B/5689